THE ENCYCLOPEDIA OF
CROCHET TECHNIQUES

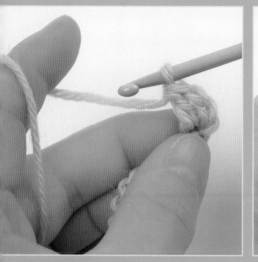

THE ENCYCLOPEDIA OF
CROCHET TECHNIQUES

A unique visual directory of crochet techniques
plus an inspirational gallery of finished pieces

JAN EATON

SEARCH PRESS

A QUARTO BOOK

Published in 2006 by Search Press Ltd
Wellwood
North Farm Road
Tunbridge Wells
Kent TN2 3DR
United Kingdom

Reprinted 2007, 2008 (twice), 2009 (twice), 2010 (twice)

ISBN: 978-1-84448-141-5

A catalogue record for this book is available from the British
Library

Conceived, designed and produced by
Quarto Publishing plc
The Old Brewery
6 Blundell Street
London N7 9BH

QUAR: ECR

Project Editor: Lindsay Kaubi
Art Editor and Designer: Julie Francis
Assistant Art Director: Penny Cobb
Illustrators: Kuo Kang Chen, Coral Mula
Symbol Charts: Betty Barnden
Photographers: Phil Wilkins, Martin Norris
Copy Editors: Pauline Hornsby, Helen Jordan
Proofreader: Diana Chambers
Picture Research: Claudia Tate
Indexer: Diana LeCore

Art Director: Moira Clinch
Publisher: Paul Carslake

Manufactured by PICA Digital, Singapore
Printed by Toppan Leefung Printing Ltd, China

CONTENTS

ABOUT THIS BOOK

The book begins with Crochet Essentials, a chapter packed with the basics of crochet. Once you've mastered the basics, move on to the Techniques and Stitches chapter, which will expand your knowledge and skills. Each technique is self-contained so you can dip in and out of the book as you like or work your way from beginning to end. The Projects and Gallery chapters will encourage you to put into practice the skills you have learned.

CROCHET ESSENTIALS

Crochet Essentials guides you step-by-step through all the crochet basics in easy-to-follow sequences: from equipment and materials and how to hold the hook and yarn to basic stitches, how to read patterns and how to stitch seams. This course in the essentials will direct you through your first steps in crochet.

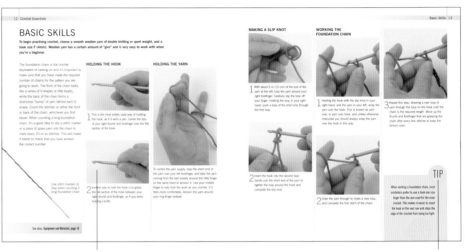

Step-by-step sequences and clear, easy-to-follow illustrations accompany each skill.

Useful tips are scattered throughout the book.

PROJECTS

There are seven attractive projects in the book, ranging from a simple scarf worked in a pretty lace stitch to a gorgeous striped purse crocheted entirely in the round using a selection of contrasting yarns. All of the projects encourage you to use and expand on the techniques you've already learnt.

Each project is illustrated with an inspirational picture of the finished item.

Clear instructions list materials, tension, finished size and how to make up the item.

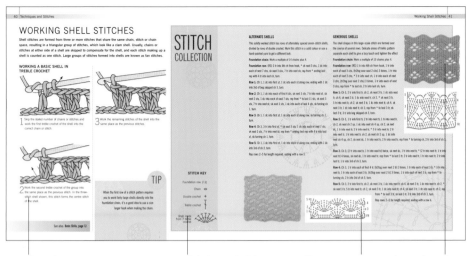

Step-by-step sequences explain how to work the stitch.

Stitch symbol key explains the symbols used in the pattern.

Patterns are written and charted.

A crocheted sample shows the finished fabric.

TECHNIQUES AND STITCHES

From the easiest of striped patterns to the lacy delights of filet crochet, the Techniques and Stitches section progresses through a wide range of crochet stitches and techniques beginning with simple patterns and shapes. It then moves on to textured stitches and non-standard techniques such as hairpin and Tunisian crochet, and finally, explains how to make embellishments like cords and trims, and how to add beads and sequins. Each technique is accompanied by a Stitch Collection to encourage you to put the technique you have just mastered into practise.

Each item is described in full with useful information on how it was created.

Vibrant colour pictures provide inspiration and ideas for colour schemes, stitches, and possibilities for your own projects.

GALLERY

This section showcases some of the different ways of using crochet fabric from making toys for children to creating stylish garments and one-off designer textiles. Crochet fabric is a textile with a huge range of possibilities; it can be light, delicate and lacy, chunky and textured, smooth and patterned in a variety of ways. Organized into sub categories such as garments, jewellery, bags and toys, you can dip into the gallery anywhere for instant inspiration.

Resources

The Resources holds detailed information on the abbreviations and stitch symbols used in the book, plus recommendations on standard hook and yarn combinations.

A handy Glossary gives quick definitions of the terms used throughout the book and there's a list of suppliers for crochet materials.

Chapter 1
CROCHET ESSENTIALS

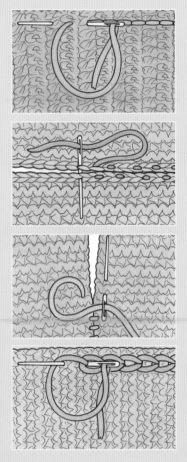

This chapter contains all the key skills
you need to get started with crochet.
From choosing yarn and hooks to
working the basic stitches and
understanding both written and
charted crochet patterns, this is the
place to start, whether you are a
beginner or someone who wants to
freshen up existing crochet skills.

EQUIPMENT AND MATERIALS

To take up crochet, all you need is a crochet hook and a ball of yarn. Hooks are available in a wide range of sizes and materials, and yarn also comes in a wide variety of materials, weights, colours and price ranges. It is important to choose the right yarn for your project.

HOOKS

Hooks from different manufacturers, and those made from different materials can vary widely in shape and size even though they may all be branded with the same number or letter to indicate their size. Although the hook sizes quoted in pattern instructions are a very useful guide, you may find that you need to use smaller or larger hook sizes, depending on the brand, to achieve the correct tension for a pattern. The most important thing to consider when choosing a hook is how it feels in your hand, and the ease with which it works with your yarn.

When you have discovered your perfect brand of hook, it's useful to buy a range of several different sizes so that they are always available to you. Store your hooks in a clean container such as a cosmetic bag. If the hook you are using starts to feel greasy or sticky, wash it in warm water with a little detergent, rinse with clean water and dry thoroughly.

A selection of aluminium, plastic, bamboo and resin hooks.

▲ ▶ COMMON HOOKS
The most common types of hooks are made from aluminium or plastic and they come in a wide range of sizes to suit different yarn weights. Hand-made wooden and horn hooks are also available, many featuring decorative handles.

Small hooks

▶ SMALL HOOKS
Small sizes of steel hooks are also made for working crochet with fine cotton yarns (this type of fine work is often called thread crochet) and they often have plastic handles to give a better grip.

◀ SPECIALIZED HOOKS
Specialist hooks with easy-to-hold handles are useful additions to a hook collection, as are double-ended hooks with a different size of hook at each end.

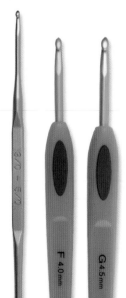

Specialized hooks

TIP

Useful hook/yarn combinations
Sport weight (4 ply) B–E
(2.5 mm–3.5 mm)
Double knitting (DK) E–G
(3.5 mm–4.5 mm)
Worsted weight (Aran) I–J
(5 mm–6 mm)

YARNS

There are a huge range of yarns available to use for crochet, from very fine cotton to chunky wool. Yarns can be made from one fibre or combine a mixture of two or three different ones in varying proportions. As a general rule, the easiest yarns to use for crochet, especially for a beginner, have a smooth surface and a medium or tight twist.

Woolen yarns and blended yarns with a high proportion of wool feel good to crochet with as they have a certain amount of stretch, making it easy to push the point of the hook into each stitch. Silk yarn has a delightful lustre, but it has less resilience than either wool or cotton and is much more expensive. Yarns made from cotton and linen are durable and cool to wear, but may be blended with other fibres to add softness. Yarns made wholly from synthetic fibres, such as acrylic or nylon, are usually less expensive to buy than those made from natural fibres, but can pill when worn and lose their shape. A good solution is to choose a yarn with a small proportion of synthetic fibres that has been combined with a natural fibre, such as wool or cotton.

Yarn is sold by weight, rather than by length, although the packaging of many yarns now includes the length per ball as well as the weight. Yarn is usually packaged in balls although some yarns may come in the form of hanks or skeins, which need to be wound by hand into balls before you can begin to crochet.

Yarns can be made from either natural or synthetic fibres, or both.

Needle case

Bent-tip yarn needles

Straight-tip yarn needles

Large-headed pins

Tape measures

Sharp scissors

▶ YARN NEEDLES

Yarn needles have blunt points, which may be straight or bent, and long eyes. They come in a range of sizes and are used for weaving-in yarn ends, and for sewing pieces of crochet together.

▶ PINS

Pins with large round or shaped heads are good for pinning crochet pieces together as the heads are easy to see and won't slip through the crochet fabric.

▶ TAPE MEASURE

Choose one that shows both centimetres and inches on the same side and replace it when it becomes worn or frayed. A worn tape measure will probably have stretched and become inaccurate.

▼ SHARP SCISSORS

Choose a small, pointed pair of scissors to cut yarn and trim off yarn ends.

BASIC SKILLS

To begin practising crochet, choose a smooth woollen yarn of double knitting or sport weight, and a hook size F (4mm). Woollen yarn has a certain amount of "give" and is very easy to work with when you're a beginner.

The foundation chain is the crochet equivalent of casting on and it's important to make sure that you have made the required number of chains for the pattern you are going to work. The front of the chain looks like a series of V-shapes or little hearts, while the back of the chain forms a distinctive "bump" of yarn behind each V-shape. Count the stitches on either the front or back of the chain, whichever you find easier. When counting a long foundation chain, it's a good idea to slip a stitch marker or a piece of spare yarn into the chain to mark every 20 or so stitches. This will make it easier to check that you have worked the correct number.

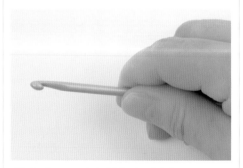

Use stitch markers to help when counting a long foundation chain.

See also: **Equipment and Materials, page 10**

HOLDING THE HOOK

1 This is the most widely used way of holding the hook, as if it were a pen. Centre the tips of your right thumb and forefinger over the flat section of the hook.

2 Another way to hold the hook is to grasp the flat section of the hook between your right thumb and forefinger, as if you were holding a knife.

HOLDING THE YARN

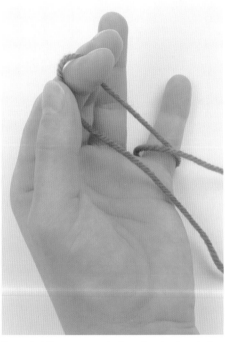

To control the yarn supply, loop the short end of the yarn over your left forefinger, and take the yarn coming from the ball loosely around the little finger on the same hand to tension it. Use your middle finger to help hold the work as you crochet. If it feels more comfortable, tension the yarn around your ring finger instead.

MAKING A SLIP KNOT

1 With about 6 in (15 cm) of the end of the yarn at the left, loop the yarn around your right forefinger. Carefully slip the loop off your finger. Holding the loop in your right hand, push a loop of the short end through the first loop.

2 Insert the hook into the second loop. Gently pull the short end of the yarn to tighten the loop around the hook and complete the slip knot.

WORKING THE FOUNDATION CHAIN

1 Holding the hook with the slip knot in your right hand, and the yarn in your left, wrap the yarn over the hook. This is known as yarn over, or yarn over hook, and unless otherwise instructed you should always wrap the yarn over the hook in this way.

2 Draw the yarn through to make a new loop, and complete the first stitch of the chain.

3 Repeat this step, drawing a new loop of yarn through the loop on the hook until the chain is the required length. Move up the thumb and forefinger that are grasping the chain after every few stitches to keep the tension even.

TIP

When working a foundation chain, most crocheters prefer to use a hook one size larger than the size used for the main crochet. This makes it easier to insert the hook on the next row and stops the edge of the crochet from being too tight.

COUNTING CHAINS

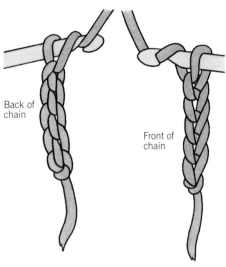

Back of chain

Front of chain

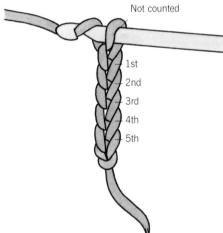

Not counted

1st
2nd
3rd
4th
5th

Count each V-shaped loop on the front of the chain as one chain stitch, except for the loop on the hook, which is not counted. You may find it easier to turn the chain over and count the stitches on the back of the chain.

WORKING INTO THE FOUNDATION CHAIN

1 You're now ready to work the first row of stitches into the chain. There are different places to insert the hook into the chain, but this way is the easiest one for the beginner, although it does give the crochet a rather loose edge. Holding the chain with the front facing you, insert the hook into the top loop of the chain and work the first stitch as stated in the pattern.

2 To make a stronger, neater edge which can stand alone, without an edge finish being needed, turn the chain so the back of it is facing you. Work the first row of stitches as instructed in the pattern, inserting the hook through the "bump" at the back of each chain stitch.

Turning chains

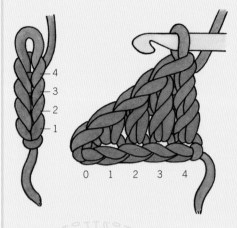

4
3
2
1

0 1 2 3 4

When working crochet in rows or rounds, you will need to work a specific number of extra chains at the beginning of each row or round. The extra chains are needed to bring the hook up to the correct height for the particular stitch you will be working next. When the work is turned at the end of a straight row, the extra chains are called a turning chain, and when they are worked at the beginning of a round, they are called a starting chain.
The diagram above shows the correct number of chain stitches needed to make a turn for each stitch. If you are inclined to work chain stitches very tightly, you may find that you need to work an extra chain in order to keep the edges of your work from becoming too tight.

Double crochet stitch	1 turning chain
Half treble crochet stitch	2 turning chains
Treble crochet stitch	3 turning chains
Double treble crochet stitch	4 turning chains

The turning or starting chain is usually counted as the first stitch of the row, except when working single crochet where the single turning chain is ignored. For example, ch 4 (counts as 1dtr) at the beginning of a row or round means that the turning or starting chain contains four chain stitches, and these are counted as the equivalent of one double treble crochet stitch. A turning or starting chain may be longer than the number required for the stitch, and in that case counts as one stitch plus a number of chains. For example, ch 6 (counts as 1dtr, ch 2) means that the turning or starting chain is the equivalent of one double treble crochet stitch plus two chain stitches.

At the end of the row or round, the final stitch is usually worked into the turning or starting chain worked on the previous row or round. The final stitch may be worked into the top chain of the turning or starting chain or into another specified stitch of the chain. For example, 1tr into 3rd of ch 3 means that the final stitch is a treble crochet stitch and it is worked into the 3rd stitch of the turning or starting chain.

WORKING A SLIP STITCH

Slip stitch is rarely used to create a crochet fabric on its own. Instead, it is used to join rounds of crochet, and to move the hook and yarn across a group of existing stitches to a new position. To work a slip stitch into the foundation chain, insert the hook from front to back under the top loop of the second chain from the hook. Wrap the yarn over the hook and draw it through both the chain and the loop on the hook. One loop remains on the hook, and one slip stitch has been worked.

TIP

When working slip stitches to close rounds of crochet or to move hook and yarn to a new position, take care not to work the slip stitches too tightly as this will pucker the crochet fabric.

WORKING A DOUBLE CROCHET STITCH

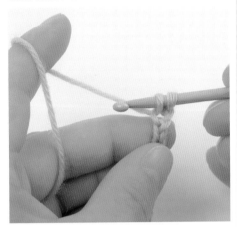

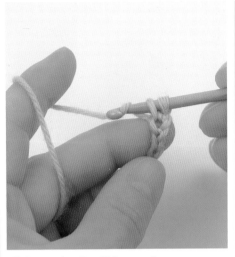

1 Work the foundation chain and insert the hook from front to back under the top loop of the second chain from the hook. Wrap the yarn over the hook and draw it through the first loop, leaving two loops on the hook.

2 To complete the stitch, wrap the yarn over the hook and draw it through both loops on the hook. Continue in this way along the row, working one double crochet stitch into each chain.

4 Insert the hook from front to back under both loops of the first double crochet at the beginning of the row. Work a double crochet stitch into each stitch of the previous row, being careful to work the final double crochet stitch into the last stitch of the row below, but not into the turning chain.

Double crochet

3 At the end of the row, turn, and work one chain for the turning chain (remember this chain does not count as a stitch).

WORKING A HALF TREBLE CROCHET STITCH

1 Wrap the yarn over the hook and insert the hook from front to back into the work (if you are at the beginning of the row, insert the hook under the top loop of the third chain from the hook).

2 Draw the yarn through the chain, leaving three loops on the hook.

3 Wrap the yarn over the hook and draw through all three loops on the hook. One loop remains on the hook and one half treble crochet stitch has been worked.

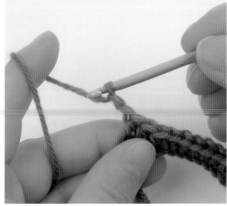

4 Continue along the row, working one half treble crochet stitch into each chain. At the end of the row, work two chains for the turning chain and turn.

5 Missing the first half treble crochet stitch at the beginning of the row, wrap the yarn over the hook, insert the hook from front to back under both loops of the second stitch on the previous row, and work a half treble crochet stitch into each stitch made on the previous row. At the end of the row, work the last stitch into the top stitch of the turning chain.

Half treble crochet

WORKING A TREBLE CROCHET STITCH

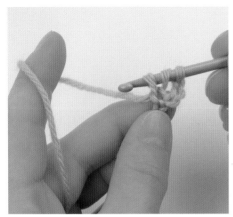

1 Wrap the yarn over the hook and insert the hook from front to back into the work (if you are at the beginning of the row, insert the hook under the top loop of the fourth chain from the hook). Draw the yarn through the chain, leaving three loops on the hook.

Treble crochet

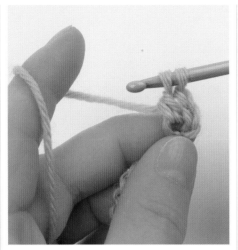

2 Wrap the yarn over the hook and draw it through the first two loops on the hook so two loops remain on the hook.

3 Wrap the yarn over the hook. Draw the yarn through the two loops on the hook. One loop remains on the hook and one treble crochet stitch has been worked.

4 At the end of the row, work three chains for the turning chain and turn.

5 Missing the first treble crochet stitch at the beginning of the row, wrap the yarn over the hook, insert the hook from front to back under both loops of the second stitch on the previous row, and work a treble crochet stitch into each stitch made on the previous row. At the end of the row, work the last stitch into the top stitch of the turning chain.

WORKING A DOUBLE TREBLE CROCHET STITCH

1 Wrap the yarn over the hook twice. Insert the hook from front to back into the work (if you are at the beginning of the row, insert the hook under the top loop of the fifth chain from the hook). Wrap the yarn over the hook and draw through, leaving four loops on the hook. Wrap the yarn over the hook again.

3 To complete the stitch, wrap the yarn over the hook again, and draw through the remaining two loops on the hook. One loop remains on the hook. Repeat along the row.

2 Working in a similar way to a treble crochet stitch (opposite), draw the yarn through two loops (three loops on the hook), wrap the yarn again, draw through two loops (two loops on the hook).

4 At the beginning of the next and every following row, work four turning chains, wrap the yarn twice over the hook and insert the hook into the second stitch of the row. At the end of every row, work the last stitch into the top stitch of the turning chain.

Double treble crochet

MEASURING TENSION

The term "tension" refers to the number of stitches and rows contained in a given width and length of crochet fabric. Crochet patterns include a recommended tension for the yarn that has been used to make the item shown. It's important that you match this tension exactly so that your work comes out the right size.

Tension measurements are usually quoted as x stitches and y rows to 10 cm (4 in) measured over a certain stitch pattern using a certain size of hook. The information may also include a measurement taken across one or more pattern repeats. Working to the suggested tension will also ensure that the crochet fabric is neither too heavy and stiff, nor too loose and floppy. Yarn ball bands or tags may also quote a recommended tension as well as giving information on fibre composition, yardage and aftercare.

Always try to use the exact yarn quoted in the pattern instructions. Two yarns of the same weight and fibre content made by different manufacturers will vary slightly in thickness.

Tension can be affected by the type of yarn used, the size and brand of the crochet hook, the type of stitch pattern and by the tension of an individual crocheter. No two people will crochet to exactly the same tension, even when working with the identical hook and yarn. How you hold the hook, and the rate at which the yarn flows through your fingers will affect the tension you produce. Crochet fabric has less "give" and elasticity than a comparable knitted fabric, so it's crucial to make and measure a tension swatch before you begin making any item. Accessories (purses, hats) and items of home furnishings (pillow covers, lace edgings) are often worked to a tighter tension than scarves, garments and afghans, which need a softer type of fabric with better drape.

MAKING AND MEASURING A TENSION SAMPLE

Read the pattern instructions to find the recommended tension. Working in the exact yarn you will use for the item, make a generously-sized sample 15–20 cm (6–8 in) wide. If you are working a stitch pattern, choose a number of foundation chains to suit the stitch repeat. Work in the required pattern until the piece is 15–20 cm (6–8 in) long. Fasten off the yarn. Block the tension sample using the method suited to the yarn composition and allow to dry.

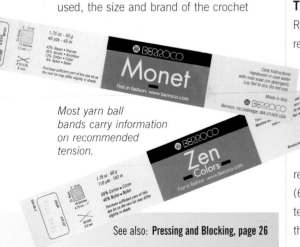

Most yarn ball bands carry information on recommended tension.

See also: **Pressing and Blocking, page 26**

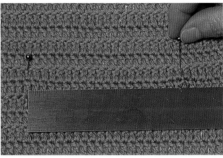

1 Lay the sample right side upwards on a flat surface and use a ruler or tape measure to measure 10 cm (4 in) horizontally across a row of stitches. Mark this measurement by inserting two pins exactly 10 cm (4 in) apart. Make a note of the number of stitches (including partial stitches) between the pins. This is the number of stitches to 10 cm (4 in).

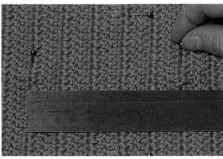

2 Turn the sample on its side. Working in the same way, measure 10 cm (4 in) across the rows, again inserting two pins exactly 10 cm (4 in) apart. Make a note of the number of rows (including partial rows) between the pins. This is the number of rows to 4 in (10 cm).

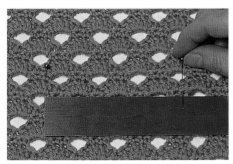

3 When working a particular stitch pattern, tension information may be quoted as a multiple of the pattern repeat, rather than as a set number of rows and stitches. Work your tension sample in pattern, but this time count repeats instead of rows and stitches between the pins.

HOW TO ADJUST THE TENSION

If you have more stitches, or a smaller pattern repeat between the pins inserted in your tension sample, your tension is too tight, and you should make another sample using a hook one size larger.

If you have fewer stitches and a larger pattern repeat between the pins inserted in your tension sample, your tension is too loose, and you should make another sample using a hook one size smaller.

Block the new sample as before, and measure the tension as above. Repeat this process until your tension matches that given in the pattern.

COMPARING TENSION

These three swatches show 20 stitches and nine rows of treble crochet worked in the same weight of yarn using different sizes of hook. As well as altering the size of the swatch, the hook also affects the drape and handle of the crochet. Swatch 1 feels hard and stiff, swatch 3 feels loose and floppy, while swatch 2 feels substantial yet still has good drape.

1 Double knitting weight yarn worked with a size C (3 mm) hook.

2 Double knitting weight yarn worked with a size F (4 mm) hook.

3 Double knitting weight yarn worked with a size I (5.5 mm) hook.

JOINING YARNS

There are a number of methods you can use to join a new ball of yarn into your crochet. The method you choose can depend on whether you are continuing in the same colour or introducing a new one.

When working all in one colour, try to join in a new ball of yarn at the end of the row rather than in the middle to make the join less noticeable. You can do this at the end of the row you are working by making an incomplete stitch, and using the new yarn to finish the stitch. Alternatively, join the new yarn at the beginning of the row you are about to work by using the slip stitch method shown below. When working colour patterns, join the new colour of yarn into the last stitch worked in the old colour using the joining in the middle of the row method shown below.

JOINING A NEW YARN IN TREBLE CROCHET

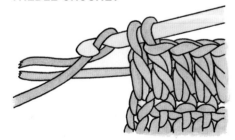

1 Join the new colour at the end of the last row worked in the previous colour. Leaving the last stage of the final stitch incomplete, loop the new yarn round the hook and pull it though the stitches on the hook to complete the stitch.

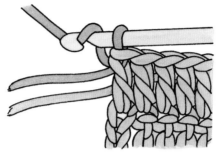

2 Turn and work the next row with the new colour. You may find it easier to knot the two loose ends together before you cut the yarn no longer in use, leaving an end of about 10 cm (4 in). Always undo the knot before weaving in the yarn ends.

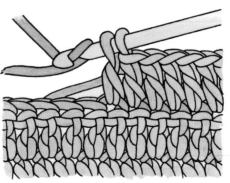

3 When working colour patterns, join the new yarn colour where the pattern or chart indicates. Leave the last stitch worked in the old colour incomplete and proceed as above.

JOINING A NEW YARN IN DOUBLE CROCHET

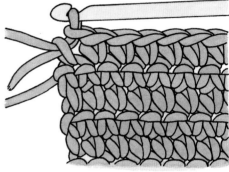

1 Join the new colour at the end of the last row worked in the previous colour. To work the last stitch, draw a loop of the old yarn through so that there are two loops on the hook, loop the new yarn round the hook, and pull it through both stitches on the hook. Turn, and work the next row with the new colour.

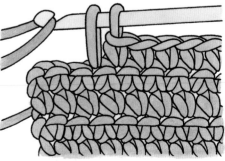

2 When working colour patterns, join the new yarn colour where the pattern or chart indicates. Leave the last stitch worked in the old colour incomplete and proceed as above.

JOINING A NEW YARN USING SLIP STITCH

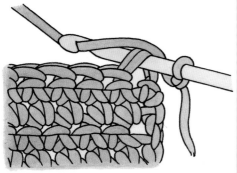

This method can be used when working any stitch. At the beginning of the row, make a slip knot in the new yarn and place it on the hook. Insert the hook into the first stitch of the row and make a slip stitch with the new yarn through both stitch and slip knot. Continue along the row using the new yarn.

FASTENING OFF YARN

It's very easy to fasten off yarn when you've finished a piece of crochet. Do remember not to cut the yarn too close to the work, as you will need enough yarn to weave in the yarn end.

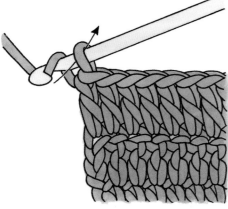

1 Cut the yarn about 15 cm (6 in) from the last stitch. Wrap the yarn over the hook and draw the yarn end through the loop on the hook.

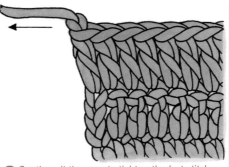

2 Gently pull the yarn to tighten the last stitch. Weave the yarn end in on the wrong side of the work as shown below.

DEALING WITH YARN ENDS

It's important to fasten off yarn ends securely so they don't unravel in wear, or during laundering. Try to do this as neatly as possible, so that the woven yarn doesn't show through on the front of the work.

WEAVING A YARN END AT THE TOP EDGE

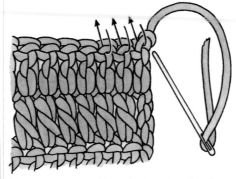

To weave a yarn end in at the top edge of a piece of crochet, start by threading the end into a yarn needle. Take the yarn through several stitches on the wrong side of the crochet, working stitch by stitch. Trim the remaining yarn.

WEAVING A YARN END AT THE LOWER EDGE

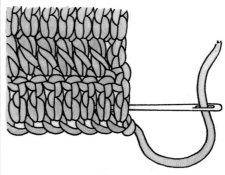

To weave a yarn end in along the lower edge of a piece of crochet, start by threading the end into a yarn needle. Draw the needle through several stitches on the wrong side of the crochet and trim the remaining yarn.

WEAVING IN YARN ENDS ON A STRIPE PATTERN

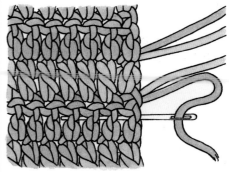

When weaving in yarn ends on a stripe pattern, or when using more than one yarn colour, it pays to take a little more care and avoid the colours showing through on the right side. Undo the knot securing the two yarn ends, thread the needle with one colour, and weave the end into the wrong side of the same colour of stripe. Repeat with the second colour.

READING PATTERNS AND CHARTS

Crochet patterns come in different forms. There's the written type where you must follow the written instructions line-by-line. The same instructions can also be shown as a symbol chart which may accompany written instructions or replace them entirely. A filet crochet design is usually shown as a black-and-white chart giving the position of the blocks and spaces which make up the design. Jacquard and intarsia patterns have their own type of charts where each stitch is represented by a block of colour, in the same way as a chart for a cross-stitch design.

UNDERSTANDING WRITTEN INSTRUCTIONS

At first sight the terminology of crochet can look rather complicated. The most important thing to remember when following a pattern is to check that you start off with the correct number of stitches in the foundation row or ring, and then work through the instructions exactly as stated.

In a written pattern, **square brackets (1)** and **asterisks (2)** are used to make written patterns shorter and to avoid tedious repetition. Instructions may be phrased slightly differently depending on whether square brackets or asterisks are used, and both may be used together in the same pattern row of a complex design. The sequence of stitches enclosed inside square brackets must be worked as instructed. For example, [1 tr into each of next 2 sts, ch 2] 3 times means that you will work the three treble crochet stitches and the two chains three times in all. The instruction may also be expressed like this: *1 tr into each of next 2 sts, ch 2; rep from * 3 times. The information is exactly the same, but it is

See also: **Filet Crochet, page 54**
Jacquard Crochet, page 66
Intarsia Crochet, page 68
Abbreviations and Symbols, page 148

CIRCLE IN A SQUARE

Yarn: Worked in one colour of yarn.

Foundation ring: Ch 6 and join with sl st to form a ring.

Round 1: Ch 3 (counts as 1 tr), work 15 tr into ring, join with sl st into 3rd of ch 3. (16 tr).

Round 2: Ch 5 (counts as 1 tr, ch 2), [1 tr into next tr, ch 2] 15 times, join with sl st into 3rd of ch 5.

Round 3: Ch 3, 2 tr into ch 2 sp, ch 1, [3 tr, ch 1] into each ch 2 sp, join with sl st into 3rd of ch 3.

Round 4: * [ch 3, 1 dc into next sp] 3 times, ch 6 (corner sp made), 1 dc into next ch 1 sp; rep from * to end, join

stated in a slightly different way. You may also find asterisks used in instructions which tell you how to work any stitches remaining after the last complete repeat of a stitch sequence is worked. For example, rep from * to end, ending with 1 tr into each of last 2 sts, turn means that you have two stitches left at the end of the row after working the last repeat. In this case, work one treble crochet stitch into each of the last two stitches before turning to begin the next row.

You'll also find **round brackets (3)** in written instructions. They usually contain extra information, not instructions which have to be worked. For example, Row 1: (RS) means that the right side of the work is facing you as you work this row. Round brackets are also used to indicate the number of different sizes in which a garment pattern is worked as well as the different

numbers of stitches. In this case, it's helpful to read right through the pattern and highlight the corresponding numbers as an aid to easy reading. You may also find a number enclosed in round brackets at the end of a row or round—this indicates the total number of stitches you have worked in that particular row or round. For example, (12 tr) at the end of a round means that you have worked 12 treble crochet stitches in the round.

Each crochet stitch pattern worked in rows is written using a specific number of pattern rows and the sequence is repeated until the piece of crochet is the correct length. When working a complicated pattern, always make a note of exactly which row you are working as it's very easy to forget exactly which row you are working on when your crochet session gets interrupted.

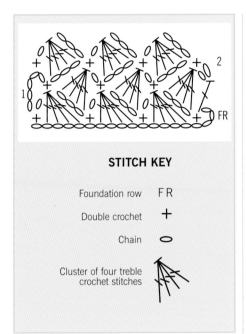

STITCH KEY

Foundation row	F R
Double crochet	+
Chain	o
Cluster of four treble crochet stitches	

READING SYMBOL CHARTS

Some crochet patterns use symbol charts to describe the method of working visually. Symbols indicate the different stitches and where and how they should be placed in relation to one another. A symbol chart will still contain some written instructions, but the stitch patterns are shown in a visual form and not written out line-by-line.

To use a symbol chart, first familiarize yourself with the different symbols. There's a list of symbols used in the symbol charts on page 148 and the symbols used in each pattern are also shown in a key at the side of the chart. Each symbol represents a single instruction or stitch and indicates where to work the stitch. Follow the numerical sequence on the chart whether you are working in rows or rounds.

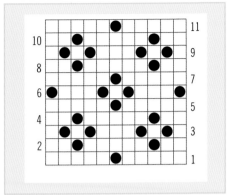

READING FILET CROCHET CHARTS

Filet crochet charts are numbered at the sides and you follow the numbered sequence upwards from the bottom of the chart, working from side to side. Each open square on the chart represents one space and each solid square represents a block.

Filet, jacquard and intarsia crochet instructions are all illustrated on grids with either coloured squares or solid and open squares.

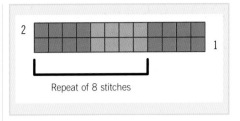

Repeat of 8 stitches

READING COLOUR BLOCK CHARTS

Jacquard and intarsia patterns are shown as a coloured chart on a grid. Each coloured square on the chart represents one stitch and you should always work upwards from the bottom of the chart, reading odd-numbered rows (right side rows) from right to left and even-numbered rows (wrong side rows) from left to right.

Begin by working the foundation chain in the first colour, then starting at the bottom right-hand corner of the chart, work the pattern from the chart, joining in new colours as they occur in the design. On the first row, work the first stitch into the second chain from the hook, then work the rest of the row in double crochet.

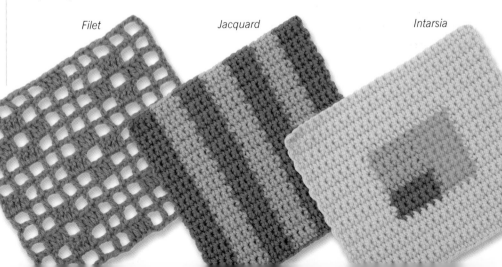

Filet   *Jacquard*   *Intarsia*

PRESSING AND BLOCKING

A light press on the wrong side with a cool iron is often all the treatment that pieces of crochet need before being stitched together, but some pieces, such as garment sections and crocheted motifs will need more attention.

The process of blocking involves easing and pinning the crocheted pieces into the correct shape on a fabric-covered board, then either steaming with an iron or moistening with cold water depending on the fibre content of your yarn. Always be guided by the information given on the ball band of your yarn as most man-made fibres are easily damaged by heat. When in doubt, choose the cold water method for blocking man-made fibres shown opposite.

Yarns made from most natural fibres (cotton, linen and wool, but not silk, which is more delicate) can be blocked with warm steam. A large item such as a blanket or throw made in one piece (or from motifs which have been joined together as you go) can be carefully pressed from the wrong side over a well-padded ironing board, using a light touch to avoid crushing the stitches. Don't steam or hot press a crochet piece made from man-made yarns such as nylon or acrylic—you will flatten it and make the yarn limp and lifeless. Instead, use a cool iron or the cold water blocking method shown opposite.

To block garment pieces and large quantities of separate motifs, it's a good idea to make your own blocking board. You can

do this inexpensively by covering a 60 x 90 cm (24 x 36 in) piece of flat board (a lightweight pinboard made from cork is ideal) with one or two layers of quilter's wadding. Secure the wadding on the back of the board with staples or thumb tacks, then cover with a layer of fabric and secure in the same way. Choose fabric made from cotton so it can withstand the heat of the iron – a check pattern is useful so the lines can help you pin out straight edges. Use plenty of rustproof pins to pin out the pieces, and make sure the pins have glass rather than plastic heads as these will melt when heat is applied. When pinning out long pieces such as edgings or borders, work in sections and allow each section to dry completely before moving on to the next section.

Recommended tension

Shade and dye lot numbers

Weight and length of yarn ball

Washing and pressing instructions

Fibre content of yarn

PINNING THE PIECES

Pin out the piece, inserting the pins through the fabric and wadding layers. Be generous with the amount of pins you use around the edges, and gently ease the crochet into shape before inserting each pin. Unless the piece is heavily textured and needs blocking face-up, you can block crochet with either the right side or wrong side facing upwards.

TIP

If you're planning to block lots of pieces of crochet of the same size, for example, square motifs to make an afghan, it's a good idea to make a special blocking board so you can pin out six or more pieces at a time. Mark out the outlines of several squares to the correct dimensions on a piece of plain, light-coloured fabric with a pencil, allowing about 5 cm (2 in) of space between the squares for ease of pinning. Use the fabric to cover a blocking board as described left.

BLOCKING NATURAL FIBRES

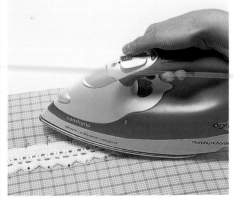

To block natural fibre yarns, hold a steam iron set at the correct temperature for the yarn about 2 cm (¾ in) above the surface of the crochet and allow the steam to penetrate for several seconds. Work in sections and don't allow the iron to come into contact with the crochet surface. Lay the board flat and allow the crochet to dry before removing the pins.

BLOCKING MAN-MADE FIBRES

To block man-made fibre yarns, pin out the pieces as above, then use a spray bottle to mist the crochet with clean cold water until it is evenly moist all over, but not saturated. When blocking heavyweight yarns, gently pat the crochet with your hand to help the moisture penetrate more easily. Lay the board flat and allow the crochet to dry before removing the pins.

SEAMS

There are several methods of joining pieces of crochet by sewing or using a crochet hook. Use the same yarn for both crochet fabric and seams, unless your yarn is thick or textured, in which case use a finer yarn of matching colour.

A back stitch, chain stitch or slip stitch seam is durable and good for joining irregular edges, but can be rather bulky depending on the weight of the yarn. These methods are good for seaming loose-fitting garments such as winter sweaters and jackets. A woven seam gives a flatter finish as straight edges are joined edge to edge. This method works better for occasions when you're making up fine work and baby garments. Double crochet seams are good for joining straight edges as they are less bulky than the first three methods mentioned above. Double crochet seams can also be used on the right side of a garment – work the seams in contrasting yarn to make a decorative statement. The last two crochet methods, double crochet and chain seam, and alternating slip stitch seam, give a flatter effect than the crochet methods mentioned above, and have the advantage of being slightly stretchy.

See also: **Basic Skills, page 12**

BACK STITCH SEAM

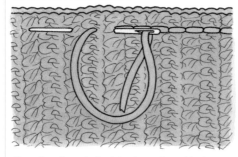

Place the pieces to be joined together with the right sides facing and pin together, inserting the pins at right angles to the edge. Thread a yarn needle with matching yarn and work a row of back stitch from right to left, one or two stitches away from the edge.

CHAIN STITCH SEAM

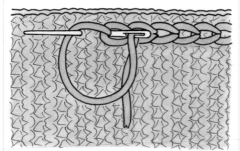

This is the stitched version of the slip stitch seam shown right. Place the pieces to be joined together with the right sides facing and pin together, inserting the pins at right angles to the edge. Thread a yarn needle with matching yarn and work a row of chain stitches from right to left close to the edge.

WOVEN SEAM

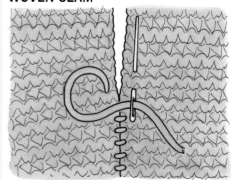

Place the pieces to be joined side by side on a flat surface with the wrong side facing upwards and the row ends touching. Thread a yarn needle with matching yarn and work a vertical row of evenly-spaced stitches in a loose zigzag pattern from edge to edge, carefully tightening the tension of the stitches as you work so the edges pull together. For double crochet, pick up one stitch; for treble crochet, pick up half a stitch.

JOINING UPPER EDGES

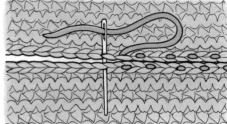

Place the pieces to be joined side by side on a flat surface with the wrong side facing upwards and the top edges touching. Thread a yarn needle with matching yarn and work a horizontal row of evenly-spaced stitches through the chains. Work from edge to edge, tightening the tension of the stitches as you work so the edges pull together.

SLIP STITCH SEAM

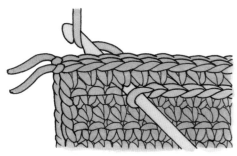

This is the crochet version of the chain stitch seam shown left. Place the pieces to be joined together with the right sides facing and pin together, inserting the pins at right angles to the edge. Holding the yarn behind the work, insert the hook through both layers of fabric, draw a loop of yarn through both layers of fabric, and loop onto the hook. Repeat, working from right to left. Secure the yarn end carefully as slip stitch can unravel easily.

DOUBLE CROCHET SEAM

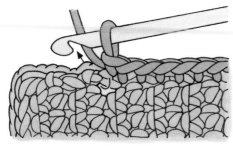

Place the pieces to be joined together with the right sides facing for a concealed seam, or wrong sides facing for a decorative seam. Pin the layers together, inserting the pins at right angles to the edge. Holding the yarn behind the work, insert the hook through both layers of fabric and work a row of double crochet stitches close to the edge. Space the stitches so that the work remains flat without stretching or puckering.

DOUBLE CROCHET ACROSS UPPER EDGES

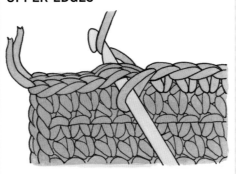

Place the pieces to be joined together with the wrong sides facing and the top edges aligned. Pin the layers together, inserting the pins at right angles to the edge. Holding the yarn behind the work, insert the hook through corresponding chains on both layers and work a row of double crochet stitches through the chains.

DOUBLE CROCHET AND CHAIN SEAM

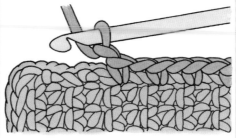

Place the pieces to be joined together with the right sides facing and pin together, inserting the pins at right angles to the edge. Holding the yarn behind the work, insert the hook through both layers of fabric, and work a double crochet stitch at the beginning of the seam. Work a chain, then another double crochet stitch a short distance from the first. Repeat evenly along the edge, alternating double crochet stitches and chains, and ending with a double crochet stitch.

ALTERNATING SLIP STITCH SEAM

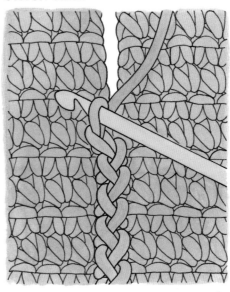

Place the pieces to be joined side by side on a flat surface with the wrong side facing upwards and the row ends touching. Work a slip stitch at the bottom corner of the right-hand piece, then work another in the corresponding stitch on the left-hand piece. Continue to work slip stitches along the seam, alternating from side to side.

TIP

It's a good idea to try out some of the seams shown here before you start assembling a project. Crochet a couple of samples in your project stitch and use contrasting yarn so you can easily unpick the seam if you don't like the effect and try a different method.

Chapter 2
TECHNIQUES AND STITCHES

The Techniques and Stitches chapter takes you through more advanced crochet techniques including working in the round, colourwork, filet crochet and making a range of sew-on trims, borders and edgings. Throughout the chapter, you'll also find Stitch Collections containing swatches, written and charted instructions for a variety of openwork, lace and textured stitch patterns.

WORKING STRIPE PATTERNS

Working stripes of colour is the easiest way to add pattern to a piece of crochet worked in one of the basic stitches. Simple horizontal stripes worked in two, three or more colours add zing to a plain garment or accessory.

Stripes can be strongly contrasting in colour or a more subtle effect can be achieved by using shades of one colour, or one basic colour plus one or more coordinating colours. Double crochet, half treble crochet and treble crochet all look good worked in stripes.

Working magic stripes is a fun way of using up the odds and ends of yarn that are left over from making other projects. You can use any short lengths of yarn, depending on the width of crochet fabric you are making, but magic stripes look best when the colour changes at least once on every row. Choose yarns of similar weight and fibre composition when making garments, but for accessories and pillow covers you can combine different weights and textures.

WORKING STRIPES WITHOUT BREAKING OFF YARN

Instead of breaking off each colour of yarn when you change to another one, you can carry the colours not in use up the side of the work when working some stripe patterns. As well as being faster, this means you have less yarn ends to deal with when you finish crocheting. You can do this when working a stripe pattern with an even number of rows using two colours.

See also: **Basic Skills, page 12**
Joining Yarns, page 22

WORKING NARROW STRIPES WITHOUT BREAKING OFF YARN

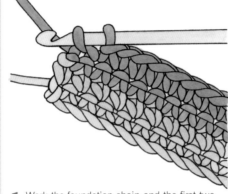

1 Work the foundation chain and the first two rows using colour A. Change to colour B without breaking yarn A and work to the last stitch, leaving two loops of yarn B on the hook.

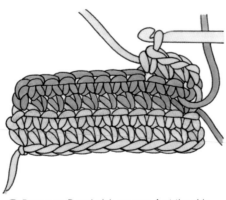

2 Drop yarn B and pick up yarn A at the side of the work. Complete the stitch with yarn A, turn, and work the next two rows using yarn A.

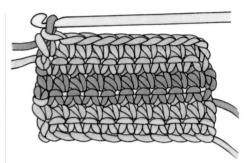

3 At the end of the second row in yarn A, drop yarn A and continue working with yarn B. Repeat the two-row stripes, alternating the yarn colours.

WORKING WIDE STRIPES WITHOUT BREAKING OFF YARN

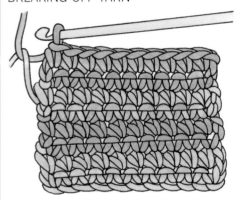

When working patterns of wider stripes which have an even number of rows, carry the colour not in use up the side of the work, but twist the two yarns together every two rows to avoid making big loops at the edge.

STITCH COLLECTION

RANDOM STRIPES

Worked in rows of half treble crochet stitches, the stripes are worked in different widths and arranged in a totally random colour sequence. Work several rows in yarn A, then continue working in the same stitch, changing colours randomly, after one, two, three or more rows have been worked.

REPEATING STRIPES

Worked in rows of double crochet stitches, the stripes are of different widths and arranged in a repeating pattern. Work two rows in yarn A, four in yarn B, four in yarn C and two in yarn D, then repeat the colour sequence from the beginning. This type of arrangement is also called a sequenced stripe pattern.

MAGIC STRIPES

Begin by winding all the yarn lengths into balls and knotting the ends together about 2 cm (¾ in) from the end and mixing colours at random. Work in rows of treble crochet stitches, pushing the knots through to the wrong side as you work. You can use either side of the crochet fabric as your right side.

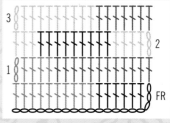

STITCH KEY

Foundation row	F R
Chain	o
Double crochet	+
Half treble crochet	T
Treble crochet	⊤
Change colour	◆

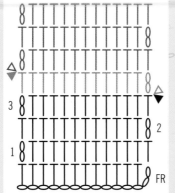

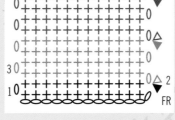

This pattern is just a suggestion for how you might work your magic stripes. You can change colours and textures wherever you want.

WORKING RIDGED STITCHES

Unless specific pattern details instruct you otherwise, it's usual to work most crochet stitches by taking the hook under both loops of the stitches made on the previous row. By working under just one loop, either the back or the front loop of a stitch, the unworked loop becomes a horizontal ridge, and the character and appearance of even the most basic crochet fabric changes.

STITCH COLLECTION

WORKING INTO THE FRONT LOOP OF DOUBLE CROCHET

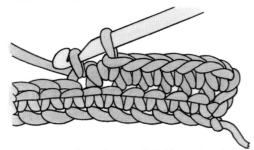

To work into the front of a row of double crochet stitches, insert the hook only under the front loops of the stitches on the previous row.

WORKING INTO THE BACK LOOP OF DOUBLE CROCHET

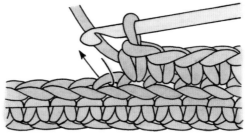

Working into the back loop of the stitch on double crochet creates a strongly-ridged fabric. To work into the back of a row of stitches, insert the hook only under the back loops of the stitches on the previous row.

WORKING INTO THE FRONT LOOP OF TREBLE CROCHET

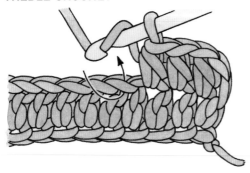

Work in the same way as for double crochet. The ridges produced on treble crochet are less pronounced than those on double crochet.

WORKING INTO THE BACK LOOP OF TREBLE CROCHET

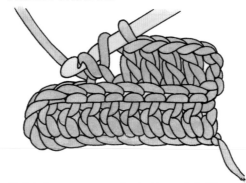

Work in the same way as for double crochet. When working a plain piece of treble crochet into either the back or front loops of each stitch, you may find that the edges of the fabric become unstable and stretchy. To prevent this, try working into both loops of the first and last stitches on every row.

See also: **Basic Skills, page 12**

STITCH KEY

Foundation row	F R
Chain	o
Double crochet	+
Treble crochet	⊦
Treble crochet in front loop	⊦
Treble crochet in back loop	⊦
Double crochet in front loop	⊥
Double crochet in back loop	⊥

WIDE RIDGES

This stitch pattern has a ridged right side and smooth wrong side. The ridged side has fairly subtle ridges which are spaced widely apart.

Foundation chain: Work over any number of chains plus 3.

Foundation row: (RS) 1 tr into 4th ch from hook, 1 tr into each ch to end, turn.

Row 1: Ch 3, 1 tr into front loop of each rem tr of previous row, ending with 1 tr into 3rd of ch 3, turn.

Row 2: Ch 3, 1 tr into both loops of rem each tr of previous row, ending with 1 tr into 3rd of ch 3, turn. Rep rows 1 & 2 for length required, ending with a row 1.

FAUX RIBBING

This stitch looks rather like knitted ribbing and both sides are identical. It can be worked in narrow bands to edge cuffs and hems on a crochet garment, or used as a textured pattern stitch in its own right.

Foundation chain: Work over any number of chains plus 1.

Foundation row: 1 dc into 2nd ch from hook, 1 dc into each ch to end, turn.

Row 1: Ch 1, 1 dc into back loop of each dc of previous row, turn.

Rep row 1 for length required.

SIMPLE RIDGES

Easily worked by alternating rows of treble and double crochet worked into the front or back loops. This stitch pattern has a ridged right side and smooth wrong side. Choose which side you prefer as the right side.

Foundation row: Work over any number of chains plus 3.

Foundation row: (RS) 1 tr into 4th ch from hook, 1 tr into each ch to end, turn.

Row 1: Ch 3, 1 tr into front loop of each tr of previous row, ending with 1 tr into 3rd of ch 3, turn.

Row 2: Ch 1, 1 dc into back loop of each tr of previous row, ending with 1 dc into 3rd of ch 3, turn.

Row 3: Ch 1, 1 dc into front loop of each dc of previous row, turn.

Row 4: Ch 3, 1 tr into back loop of each dc of previous row, turn.

Rep rows 1–4 for length required, ending with a row 2.

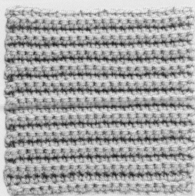

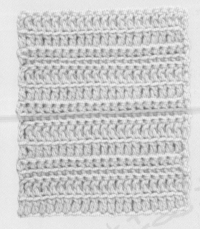

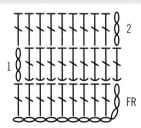

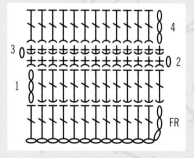

SHAPING

There are several different ways of shaping your crochet garments by increasing and decreasing the number of working stitches.

Adding or subtracting one or two stitches at intervals along a row of crochet is the easiest way; this process is known as working internal increases or decreases. When groups of stitches are added or subtracted at the beginning and end of specified rows, this is known as working external increases or decreases. The methods can be used with double, half treble, treble and double treble crochet stitches.

WORKING AN INTERNAL INCREASE

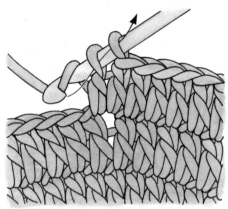

1 The simplest method of working a single increase (adding a single stitch) at intervals along a row of crochet is by working two stitches into one stitch on the previous row.

See also: **Basic Skills, page 12**

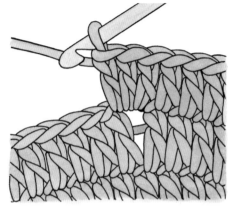

2 To work a double increase (to add two stitches) at intervals along the row, work three stitches into one stitch on the previous row.

WORKING AN EXTERNAL INCREASE

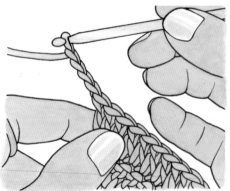

1 To increase several stitches at one time, you will need to add extra foundation chains at the appropriate end of the row.

To add stitches at the beginning of a row, work the required number of extra chains at the end of the previous row. Don't forget to add the correct number of turning chains for the stitch you are using.

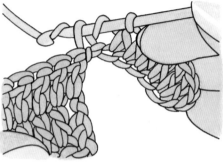

2 Turn and work back along the extra chains, then work the row in the usual way.

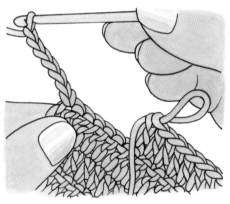

3 To add stitches at the end of a row, leave the last few stitches of the row unworked. Remove the hook. Join a length of yarn to the last stitch of the row and work the required number of extra chains, then fasten off the yarn. Insert the hook back into the row and continue, working extra stitches across the chains. Turn and work the next row in the usual way.

WORKING AN INTERNAL DECREASE

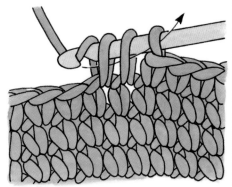

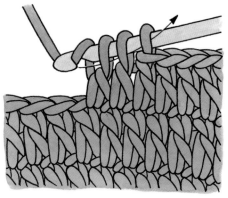

1 Decrease one double crochet stitch by working two stitches together (known as dc2tog). Leave the first stitch incomplete so there are two loops on the hook, then draw the yarn through the next stitch so you have three loops on the hook. Yarn over and pull through all three loops to finish the decrease. Two stitches can be decreased in the same way by working three stitches together (dc3tog).

2 Decrease one treble crochet stitch by working two stitches together (known as tr2tog). Leave the first stitch incomplete so there are two loops on the hook, then work another incomplete stitch so you have three loops on the hook. Yarn over and pull through all three loops to finish the decrease. Two stitches can be decreased in the same way by working three treble crochet stitches together (tr3tog).

▼ Working dc3tog at the centre of every row creates a neat square of double crochet.

WORKING AN EXTERNAL DECREASE

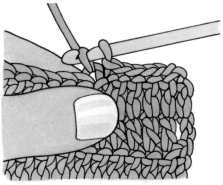

To decrease several stitches at one time at the beginning of a row, turn, work a slip stitch into each of the stitches to be decreased, then work the appropriate turning chain and continue along the row. At the end of the row, simply leave the stitches to be decreased unworked, turn, work the appropriate turning chain and continue along the row.

MAKING A NEAT EDGE

To make a neat edge at the start of a row, work the first stitch and then work the increase. At the end of the row, work until two stitches remain (the last stitch will probably be the turning chain from the previous row). Work the increase into the penultimate stitch, then work the last stitch as usual.

▲ External increases and decreases are used to add or subtract groups of stitches at the beginning and end of rows.

◀ Internal increases and decreases are used at the beginning and end of rows to shape garment edges.

WORKING CLUSTERS

Clusters are groups of two, three or more stitches that are joined together at the top by leaving the last loop of each stitch on the hook, then drawing the yarn through all the loops to secure the stitch. This technique is used as a way of decreasing one or more stitches but single, treble crochet clusters are also used to make attractive stitch patterns in their own right.

STITCH COLLECTION

WORKING A BASIC TREBLE CROCHET CLUSTER

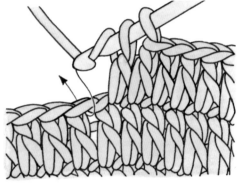

1 To work a two treble crochet cluster, yarn over hook, work the first stitch, omitting the last stage to leave two loops on the hook.

3 Wrap the yarn over the hook, draw the yarn through all three loops on the hook to complete the cluster and secure the loops.

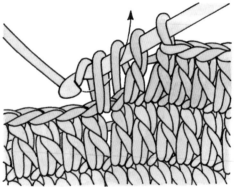

2 Work the last stitch of the cluster in the same way, resulting in three loops on the hook. Wind the yarn over the hook.

TIP

Clusters come in different sizes as they can be worked over two, three or more stitches. Try practising two-stitch clusters first, then move on to making larger ones when you've got the hang of the two-stitch ones.

See also: Shaping, page 36

STITCH KEY

Foundation row	F R
Double crochet	+
Chain	o
Cluster made from 4 treble crochet	
Cluster made from 3 double crochet	

ANGLED CLUSTERS

Rows of clusters face in opposite directions, making a beautifully textured crochet fabric. To ring the changes, try working this stitch in two-row stripes of contrasting colours.

Note: CL = cluster made from four treble crochet stitches worked together (tr4tog)

Foundation chain: Work a multiple of 5 chains plus 4.

Foundation row: (RS) 1 dc into 4th ch from hook, * ch 3, CL over next 4 chs, ch 1, 1 dc into next ch; rep from * to end, turn.

Row 1: Ch 5, 1 dc into next CL, * ch 3, CL into next ch 3 sp, ch 1, 1 dc into next CL; rep from * ending last rep with ch 3, CL into next ch 3 sp, ch 1, 1 tr into last dc, turn.

Row 2: Ch 1, sk first st, 1 dc into next CL, * ch 3, CL into next ch 3 sp, ch 1, 1 dc into next CL; rep from * ending last rep with 1 dc into sp made by ch 5, turn.

Rep rows 1 & 2 for length required, ending with a row 2.

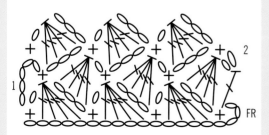

TRINITY STITCH

Trinity stitch is usually worked in one colour and the crochet fabric looks the same on the right and wrong sides, making this stitch ideal for items such as scarves where both sides can be seen.

Note: CL = cluster made from three double crochet stitches worked together (dc3tog)

Foundation chain: Work a multiple of 2 chains.

Foundation row: (WS) 1 dc into 2nd ch from hook, CL inserting hook first into same ch as previous dc, then into each of next 2 chs, * ch 1, CL inserting hook first into same ch as 3rd st of previous CL, then into each of next 2 chs; rep from * to last ch, 1 dc into same ch as 3rd st of previous CL, turn.

Row 1: Ch 1, 1 dc into first st, CL inserting hook first into same place as previous dc, then into top of next CL, then into next ch 1 sp, * ch 1, CL inserting hook first into same ch 1 sp as 3rd st of previous CL, then into top of next CL, then into next ch 1 sp; rep from * to end working 3rd st of last CL into last dc, 1 dc into same place, turn.

Rep row 1 for length required.

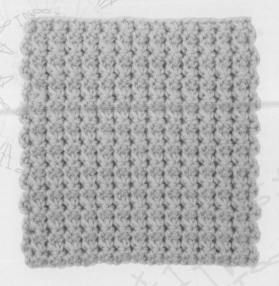

WORKING SHELL STITCHES

Shell stitches are formed from three or more stitches that share the same chain, stitch or chain space, resulting in a triangular group of stitches, which look like a clam shell. Usually, chains or stitches at either side of a shell are skipped to compensate for the shell, and each stitch making up a shell is counted as one stitch. Large groups of stitches formed into shells are known as fan stitches.

STITCH COLLECTION

WORKING A BASIC SHELL IN TREBLE CROCHET

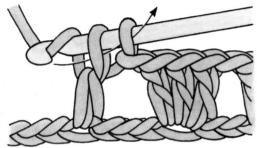

1 Skip the stated number of chains or stitches and work the first treble crochet of the shell into the correct chain or stitch.

3 Work the remaining stitches of the shell into the same place as the previous stitches.

2 Work the second treble crochet of the group into the same place as the previous stitch. In the three-stitch shell shown, this stitch forms the centre stitch of the shell.

TIP

When the first row of a stitch pattern requires you to work fairly large shells directly into the foundation chain, it's a good idea to use a size larger hook when making the chain.

See also: **Basic Skills, page 12**

STITCH KEY

Foundation row	F R
Chain	○
Double crochet	+
Treble crochet	⊤
Shell made from 7 treble crochet	

ALTERNATE SHELLS

This solidly worked stitch has rows of alternately spaced seven-stitch shells, divided by rows of double crochet. Work this stitch in a solid colour or use a hand-painted yarn to get a different look.

Foundation chain: Work a multiple of 14 chains plus 4.

Foundation row: (RS) 3 tr into 4th ch from hook, * sk next 3 chs, 1 dc into each of next 7 chs, sk next 3 chs, 7 tr into next ch; rep from * ending last rep with 4 tr into last ch, turn.

Row 1: Ch 1, 1 dc into first st, 1 dc into each st along row, ending with 1 dc into 3rd of beg skipped ch 3, turn.

Row 2: Ch 1, 1 dc into each of first 4 sts, sk next 3 sts, 7 tr into next st, sk next 3 sts, 1 dc into each of next 7 sts; rep from * to last 11 sts, sk next 3 sts, 7 tr into next st, sk next 3 sts, 1 dc into each of last 4 sts, sk turning ch 1, turn.

Row 3: Ch 1, 1 dc into first st, 1 dc into each st along row, sk turning ch 1, turn.

Row 4: Ch 3, 3 tr into first st, * sk next 3 sts, 1 dc into each of next 7 sts, sk next 3 sts, 7 tr into next st; rep from * ending last rep with 4 tr into last st, sk turning ch 1, turn.

Row 5: Ch 1, 1 dc into first st, 1 dc into each st along row, ending with 1 dc into 3rd of ch 3, turn.

Rep rows 2–5 for length required, ending with a row 5.

GENEROUS SHELLS

The shell shapes in this large-scale stitch are formed over the course of several rows. Delicate areas of trellis pattern separate each shell to give a lacy touch and lighten the effect

Foundation chain: Work a multiple of 13 chains plus 4.

Foundation row: (RS) 1 tr into 4th ch from hook, 1 tr into each of next 3 chs, [tr2tog over next 2 chs] 3 times, 1 tr into each of next 3 chs, * 3 tr into next ch, 1 tr into each of next 3 chs, [tr2tog over next 2 chs] 3 times, 1 tr into each of next 3 chs; rep from * to last ch, 2 tr into last ch, turn.

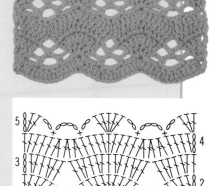

Row 1: Ch 3, 2 tr into first tr, ch 2, sk next 3 tr, 1 dc into next tr, ch 4, sk next 3 tr, 1 dc into next tr, ch 2, * sk next 3 tr, 5 tr into next tr, ch 2, sk next 3 tr, 1 dc into next tr, ch 4, sk next 3 tr, 1 dc into next tr, ch 2; rep from * to last 3 tr, sk last 3 tr, 3 tr into beg skipped ch 3, turn.

Row 2: Ch 3, 1 tr into first tr, 2 tr into next tr, 1 tr into next tr, ch 2, sk next ch 2 sp, 1 dc into next ch 4 sp, ch 2, sk next dc, 1 tr into next tr, 2 tr into next tr, * 3 tr into next tr, 2 tr into next tr, 1 tr into next tr, ch 2, sk next ch 2 sp, 1 dc into next ch 4 sp, ch 2, sk next dc, 1 tr into next tr, 2 tr into next tr; rep from * to turning ch, 2 tr into 3rd of ch 3, turn.

Row 3: Ch 3; [2 tr into next tr, 1 tr into next tr] twice, sk next dc, 1 tr into next tr, * [2 tr into next tr, 1 tr into next tr] 4 times, sk next dc, 1 tr into next tr; rep from * to last 3 tr, 2 tr into next tr, 1 tr into next tr, 2 tr into last tr, 1 tr into 3rd of ch 3, turn.

Row 4: Ch 3, 1 tr into each of first 4 tr, [tr2tog over next 2 tr] 3 times, 1 tr into each of next 3 tr, * 3 tr into next tr, 1 tr into each of next 3 tr, [tr2tog over next 2 tr] 3 times, 1 tr into each of next 3 tr; rep from * to turning ch, 2 tr into 3rd of ch 3, turn.

Row 5: Ch 3, 2 tr into first tr, ch 2, sk next 3 tr, 1 dc into next tr, ch 4, sk next 3 tr, 1 dc into next tr, ch 2, * sk next 3 tr, 5 tr into next tr, ch 2, sk next 3 tr, 1 dc into next tr, ch 4, sk next 3 tr, 1 dc into next tr, ch 2; rep from * to last 3 tr, sk last 3 tr, 3 tr into 3rd of ch 3, turn.

Rep rows 2–5 for length required, ending with a row 4.

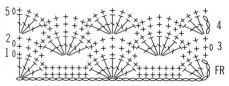

WORKING BOBBLES

A bobble is a group of stitches, usually treble crochet stitches, worked into the same stitch at the base and closed at the top. When calculating yarn requirements for a project, remember that bobbles use up more yarn than most other stitches.

Made from three, four or five stitches, bobbles are usually worked on wrong side rows, and surrounded by flat, solidly worked stitches to throw them into high relief.

WORKING A BASIC FIVE-STITCH BOBBLE

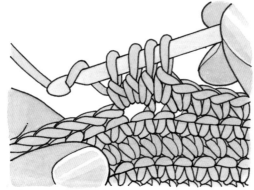

1 On a wrong side row, work to the position of the bobble. Wrap the yarn over the hook, work the first stitch, omitting the last stage to leave two loops on the hook. Work the second and third stitches in the same way. You now have four loops on the hook.

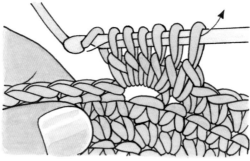

2 Work the remaining two stitches of the bobble in the same way, resulting in six loops on the hook.

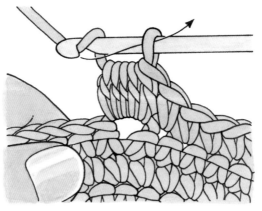

3 Wrap the yarn over the hook and draw it through all six loops to secure them and complete the bobble. You may find it helpful to gently poke the bobble through to the right side with the tip of one finger as you draw the securing loop through.

TIP

When working the following right side row, take care to work one stitch into the securing stitch at the top of each bobble.

STITCH COLLECTION

STITCH KEY

Foundation row	F R
Chain	⌀
Double crochet	+
Treble crochet	⊤
Bobble made from 4 treble crochets	
Direction of working	→

ALL-OVER BOBBLES

Four-stitch bobbles set against a double crochet background work up into a wonderfully textured piece of crochet. This type of stitch is good for making home furnishings such as pillow covers as the fabric is substantial and will keep its shape well.

Note: MB = make bobble from four treble crochet stitches.

Foundation chain: Work a multiple of 3 chains.

Foundation row: (WS) 1 dc into 2nd ch from hook, 1 dc into each ch to end, turn.

Row 1: (RS) Ch 1, 1 dc into each dc to end, turn.

Row 2: (WS) Ch 1, 1 dc into each of first 2 dc, * MB, 1 dc into each of next 2 dc; rep from * to end, turn.

Row 3: Ch 1, 1 dc into each st to end, turn.

Row 4: Ch 1, 1 dc into each dc to end, turn.

Rep rows 1–4 for length required, ending with a row 4.

ALTERNATE BOBBLES

Make a softer feeling fabric by working a row of treble crochet stitches between the bobble rows instead of the more usual double crochet. To make a flatter fabric, simply work three stitches for each bobble instead of four.

Note: MB = make bobble from four treble crochet stitches.

Foundation chain: Work a multiple of 4 chains plus 3.

Foundation row: (RS) 1 tr into 4th ch from hook, 1 tr into each ch to end, turn.

Row 1: (WS) Ch 1, 1 dc into each of first 2 tr, * MB, 1 dc into each of next 3 tr; rep from * to last 3 sts, MB, 1 dc into next tr, 1 dc into 3rd of beg skipped ch 3, turn.

Rows 2 & 4: Ch 3 (counts as 1 tr), sk first st, 1 tr into each st to end, turn.

Row 3: Ch 1, 1 dc into each of first 4 tr, * MB, 1 dc into each of next 3 tr; rep from * ending by working 1 tr into 3rd of ch 3, turn.

Row 5: Ch 1, 1 dc into each of first 2 sts, * MB, 1 dc into each of next 3 tr; rep from * to last 3 sts, MB, 1 dc into next tr, 1 dc into 3rd of ch 3, turn.

Rep rows 2–5 for length required, ending with a row 4.

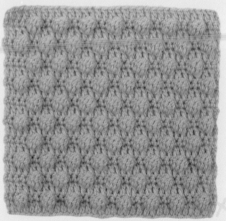

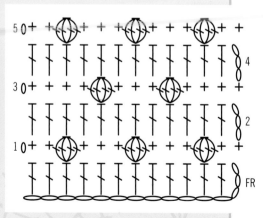

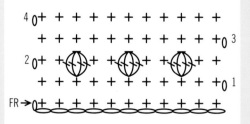

WORKING POPCORNS

A popcorn stitch is a cluster of three, four or five treble crochet stitches that is folded over and closed at the top with a chain. The popcorn looks like a tiny folded pocket, which sticks out on the right side of the crochet fabric, to give a highly textured effect.

WORKING A BASIC POPCORN STITCH

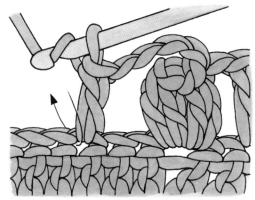

1 Work a group of five treble crochet stitches into the same chain or stitch.

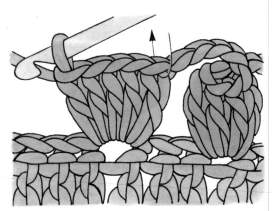

2 Remove the hook from the working loop and insert it under both loops of the first treble crochet stitch in the group.

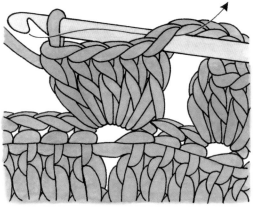

3 To close the popcorn, pick up the working loop with the hook and draw it through to fold the group of stitches and close it at the top. Secure the popcorn by wrapping the yarn over the hook and drawing it through the loop on the hook.

TIP

If you crochet tightly, you may find it easier to use a size smaller hook to work steps 2 and 3, changing back to the usual size for working the group of treble crochet stitches.

See also: **Basic Skills, page 12**

STITCH COLLECTION

STITCH KEY

Foundation row	F R
Chain	o
Double crochet	+
Treble crochet	⊤
Popcorn of 5 treble crochet	

LACY POPCORNS

This stitch sets vertical rows of single popcorns against a pretty, lacy background, and looks good worked in lighter weights of yarn, which will accentuate the delicate structure.

Note: PC = popcorn made from five treble crochet stitches.

Foundation chain: Work a multiple of 8 chains plus 2.

Foundation row: (RS) 1 dc into 2nd ch from hook, * ch 1, sk 3 chs, [1 tr, ch 1, 1 tr, ch 1, 1 tr] into next ch, sk 3 chs, 1 dc into next ch; rep from * to end, turn.

Row 1: Ch 6 (counts as 1 tr, ch 3), sk 1 tr, 1 dc into next tr, * ch 3, PC into next tr, ch 3, sk 1 tr, 1 dc into next tr; rep from * to last dc, ch 3, 1 tr into last dc, turn.

Row 2: Ch 1, 1 dc into first tr, * ch 1, [1 tr, ch 1, 1 tr, ch 1, 1 tr] into next dc, ch 1, 1 dc into top of next PC; rep from * to end working last dc into 3rd of ch 6, turn.

Rep rows 1 & 2 for length required, ending with a row 2.

POPCORN COLUMNS

Popcorn columns is a much heavier stitch than the previous one, but still makes a crochet fabric with good drape. Use this stitch for making throws and afghans where you need a textured surface.

Note: PC = popcorn made from five treble crochet stitches.

Foundation chain: Work a multiple of 11 chains plus 5.

Foundation row: (RS) 1 tr into 4th ch from hook, 1 tr into next ch, * ch 2, sk next 3 chs, PC into next ch, ch 1, PC into next ch, ch 1, sk next 2 chs, 1 tr into each of next 3 chs; rep from * to end, turn.

Row 1: Ch 3, sk first tr, 1 tr into each of next 2 tr, * ch 3, sk ch 1 and next PC, 2 dc into ch 1 sp between PCs, ch 3, sk next PC and ch 2, 1 tr into each of next 3 tr; rep from * working last tr into 3rd of beg skipped ch 3, turn.

Row 2: Ch 3, sk first tr, 1 tr into each of next 2 tr, * ch 2, sk ch 3, PC into next dc, ch 1, PC into next dc, ch 1, sk ch 3, 1 tr into each of next 3 tr; rep from * working last tr into 3rd of ch 3, turn.

Row 3: Ch 3, sk first tr, 1 tr into each of next 2 tr, * ch 3, sk ch 1 and next PC, 2 dc into ch 1 sp between PCs, ch 3, sk next PC and ch 2, 1 tr into each of next 3 tr; rep from * working last tr into 3rd of ch 3, turn.

Rep rows 2 & 3 for length required, ending with a row 2.

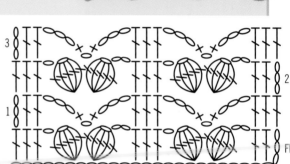

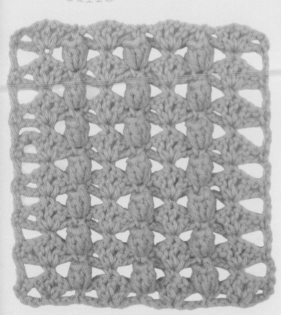

WORKING PUFF STITCHES

Puff stitches are soft, fluffy groups of stitches, which are less textured than either bobbles or popcorns. A puff stitch is made from three or more half treble crochet stitches which are worked into the same chain or stitch, and need a little practice to work successfully.

WORKING A BASIC PUFF STITCH

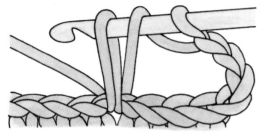

1 Wrap the yarn over the hook, insert the hook into the chain or stitch, wrap the yarn again, and draw a loop through so there are three loops on the hook.

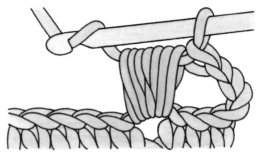

3 Wrap the yarn and draw it through the loop on the hook to close the puff stitch and secure the loops.

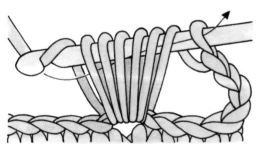

2 Repeat this step twice more, each time inserting the hook into the same place, so there are seven loops on the hook. Wrap the yarn again and draw it through all the loops on the hook.

TIP

Puff stitches can be a little tricky to work, especially for the beginner. It's a good idea to practise them using a smooth, chunky yarn and large hook until you understand the stitch construction.

See also: **Working Bobbles, page 42**
Working Popcorns, page 44

STITCH COLLECTION

STITCH KEY

Foundation row	F R
Chain	o
Double crochet	+
Half treble crochet	⊤
Treble crochet	⊤
2 treble crochet together	𝗔
Puff stitch made from 3 half treble crochet	

PUFF STITCH STRIPES

This stitch makes a softly textured crochet fabric that is perfect for making baby blankets and small afghans when worked in baby yarn. You can use either side of the work as the right side.

Note: PS = puff stitch made from 3 half treble crochet stitches.

Foundation chain: Work a multiple of 2 chains plus 2.

Foundation row: (WS) 1 dc into 2nd ch from hook, * ch 1, sk next ch, 1 dc into next ch; rep from * to end, turn.

Row 1: Ch 2 (counts as 1 htr), sk first st, * PS into next ch 1 sp, ch 1, sk 1 dc; rep from * to end, working last PS into last ch 1 sp, 1 htr into last dc, turn.

Row 2: Ch 1, 1 dc into first st, * ch 1, sk 1 st, 1 dc into next ch 1 sp; rep from * to end, working last dc into 2nd of ch 2, turn.

Rep rows 1 & 2 for length required, ending with a row 2.

PUFF STITCH WAVES

Puff stitches combined with groups of decreases make this pretty ripple pattern which looks attractive worked in a solid yarn colour or in two-row stripes of closely toning colours.

Note: PS = puff stitch made from 3 half treble crochet stitches.

tr2tog = work two treble crochet stitches together.

Foundation chain: Work a multiple of 17 chains plus 2.

Foundation row: (RS) 1 tr into 4th ch from hook, [tr2tog over next 2 chs] twice, * [ch 1, PS into next ch] 5 times, ch 1, ** [tr2tog over next 2 chs] 6 times; rep from * ending last rep at ** when 6 chs rem, [tr2tog over next 2 chs] 3 times, turn.

Row 1: Ch 1, 1 dc into first st and into each st and ch 1 sp to end of row excluding beg skipped ch 3, turn.

Row 2: Ch 3, sk first st, 1 tr into next st, [tr2tog over next 2 sts] twice, * [ch 1, PS into next st] 5 times, 1 ch, ** [tr2tog over next 2 sts] 6 times; rep from * ending last rep at ** when 6 sts rem, [tr2tog over next 2 sts] 3 times, sk ch 3, turn.

Rep rows 2 & 3 for length required, ending with a row 2.

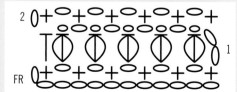

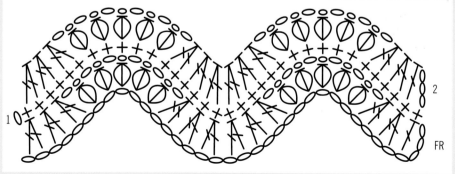

WORKING LOOP STITCHES

Loop stitches fall into two categories: the first is where extended loops are made from the working yarn (loop stitch); the second, where short lengths of crochet chain are formed into loops (astrakhan stitch). Both types of stitch make a delightful texture and are good for making accessories such as scarves and hats, or for working collars and cuffs to trim a plain garment.

WORKING A LOOP STITCH

Ordinary loop stitches are worked on wrong-side rows of double crochet by extending a loop of yarn with your finger. You'll probably need some practice before you're able to make all the loops the same size. Loop stitches can be worked in every stitch along the row, in groups or alternately with plain double crochet stitches. It's usual to work two or more plain stitches at each end of the row to make sewing seams easier.

1 With the wrong side of the work facing you, insert the hook into the next stitch as usual. Using one finger, pull up the working yarn to make a loop of the desired size, pick up both strands of the loop with the hook and draw them through the crochet fabric.

2 Take your finger out of the yarn loop and wrap the working yarn over the hook.

3 Carefully draw the yarn through all three loops on the hook

WORKING ASTRAKHAN STITCH

Unlike most other crochet stitches, astrakhan stitch is worked back and forth without turning the work. Loops of crochet chain are made on right-side rows by working into the front loops of the previous plain row. Each loop row is followed by a plain row of treble crochet stitches which are worked into the back loops of the same row as the chain loops.

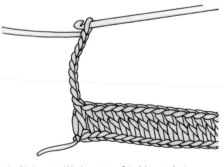

1 *Plain row:* Work a row of treble crochet stitches. At the end of the row, work the number of chains specified in the pattern. Do not turn the work.

2 *Loop row:* Working from left to right, and keeping the crochet chain behind the hook when making each loop, work a slip stitch into the front loop of the next treble crochet made on the previous row. Repeat along the row and do not turn at the end of the row.

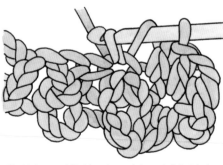

3 *Plain row:* Working from right to left behind the loops made on the previous row, work a treble crochet stitch into the back loop of each stitch made in the first plain row.

STITCH COLLECTION

BANDED LOOP STITCH

Loop stitches are worked in groups of four to make vertical bands of texture which contrast well against the plain background.

Foundation chain: Work over a multiple of 8 chains plus 2.

Foundation row: (RS) 1 tr into 4th ch from hook, 1 tr into each ch to end, turn.

Row 1: Ch 1, 1 dc into each of first 2 tr, * loop stitch into each of next 4 tr, 1 dc into each of next 4 tr; rep from * to last 6 sts, loop stitch into each of next 4 tr, 1 dc into next tr, 1 dc into 3rd of ch 3, turn.

Row 2: Ch 3, sk first st, 1 tr into each st of previous row, sk ch 1, turn.

Rep rows 1 & 2 for length required, ending with a row 1.

ASTRAKHAN STITCH

Loops of crochet chains are worked on alternate rows to create this highly textured stitch, which is worked without turning at the ends of the rows.

Foundation chain: Work over any number of chains plus 2.

Foundation row: (RS) 1 tr into 4th ch from hook, 1 tr into each ch to end. Do not turn.

Row 1: Working from left to right, sk first tr, * ch 7, sl st into front loop of next tr to right; rep from * to end, working last sl st into both loops of 3rd of beg skipped ch 3. Do not turn.

Row 2: Working from right to left behind loops made on previous row, ch 3, sk first st, * 1 tr into back loop of next tr worked on foundation row; rep from * to end. Do not turn.

Row 3: Working from left to right, * ch 7, sk first tr, sl st into front loop of next tr to right; rep from * to end, working last sl st into both loops of 3rd of ch 3. Do not turn.

Row 4: Working from right to left behind loops made on previous row, ch 3, sk first st, * 1 tr into back loop of next tr worked on last but one row; rep from * to end. Do not turn.

Rep rows 3 & 4 for length required, ending with a row 4.

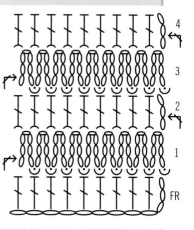

STITCH KEY

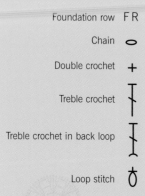

Foundation row	F R
Chain	o
Double crochet	+
Treble crochet	
Treble crochet in back loop	
Loop stitch	
Slip stitch in front loop	
Do not turn	

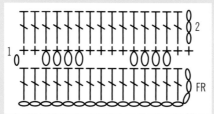

OPENWORK AND LACE STITCHES

Openwork and simple lace stitches are straightforward to work, but it's essential to work the correct number of stitches in the foundation chain. These stitches are versatile and can be used to make accessories, including shawls and wraps, as well as lightweight, simply shaped summer garments.

WORKING MESH PATTERNS

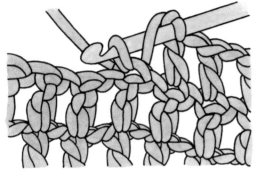

1 When working mesh patterns, take care to insert the hook into the correct place. In this pattern, the hook is inserted into the top of each stitch made on the previous row.

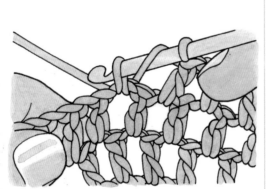

2 Some mesh patterns are made by inserting the hook into the chain spaces between stitches worked on the previous row. Don't insert the hook directly into the chain, but into the space below it.

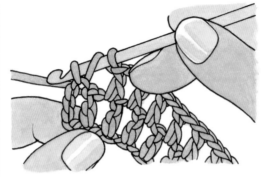

3 When working the last stitch of the row, work it into the third stitch of the turning chain rather than into the chain space. This makes a neater, more stable edge.

WORKING A TRELLIS PATTERN

Similar in construction to mesh patterns, the chain spaces in trellis patterns are longer, allowing them to curve upwards to create delicate arches. The chain spaces are usually anchored by double crochet stitches worked into the space below each arch.

See also: **Surface Cochet, page 110**

STITCH COLLECTION

STITCH KEY

Foundation row	F R
Chain	o
Double crochet	+
Treble crochet	↑
Double treble crochet	‡

OPENWORK MESH

This stitch is very easy to work and makes a good introduction to this type of stitch for the beginner. It also makes a good background stitch for surface crochet.

Foundation chain: Work a multiple of 2 chains plus 3.

Foundation row: (RS) 1 tr into 6th ch from hook, * ch 1, sk next ch, 1 tr into next ch; rep from * to end, turn.

Row 1: Ch 4 (counts as 1 tr, ch 1), * 1 tr into next tr, ch 1; rep from * to end, working last tr into 2nd of beg skipped ch 5, turn.

Row 2: Ch 4 (counts as 1 tr, ch 1), * 1 tr into next tr, ch 1; rep from * to end, working last tr into 3rd of ch 3, turn.

Rep row 2 for length required.

PLAIN TRELLIS

Another easy-to-work stitch, which is lovely when used to make a lightweight wrap, scarf or stole. It's reversible, so you can choose which side you prefer as the right side.

Foundation chain: Work over a multiple of 4 chains plus 2.

Foundation row: 1 dc into 6th ch from hook, * ch 5, sk ch 3, 1 dc into next ch; rep from * to end, turn.

Row 1: * Ch 5, 1 dc into next ch 5 sp; rep from * to end, turn.

Rep row 1 for length required.

▶ **Continued over the page**

FANCY OPENWORK

A more challenging stitch to work than either of the previous ones, the resulting crochet fabric is soft and delicate with good drape. Choose which side you prefer as the right side.

Foundation chain: Work over a multiple of 18 chains plus 8.

Foundation row: 1 tr into 8th ch from hook, * ch 2, sk next 2 chs, 1 tr into next ch; rep from * to end, turn.

Row 1: Ch 5 (counts as 1 tr, ch 2), sk first tr, 1 tr into next tr, * ch 4, 1 dtr into each of next 4 tr, ch 4, 1 tr into next tr, ch 2, 1 tr into next tr; rep from * to end, working last tr into 3rd of beg skipped ch 7, turn.

Row 2: Ch 5, sk first tr, 1 tr into next tr, * ch 4, 1 dc into each of next 4 dtr, ch 4, 1 tr into next tr, ch 2, 1 tr into next tr; rep from * to end, working last tr into 3rd of ch 5, turn.

Rows 3 & 4: Ch 5, sk first tr, 1 tr into next tr, * ch 4, 1 dc into each of next 4 dc, ch 4, 1 tr into next tr, ch 2, 1 tr into next tr; rep from * to end, working last tr into 3rd of ch 5, turn.

Row 5: Ch 5, sk first tr, 1 tr into next tr, * ch 2, [1 tr into next dtr, ch 2] 4 times, 1 tr into next tr, ch 2, 1 tr into next tr; rep from * to end, working last tr into 3rd of ch 5, turn.

Row 6: Ch 5, sk first tr, 1 tr into next tr, * ch 2, [1 dtr into next dc, ch 2] 4 times, 1 tr into next tr, ch 2, 1 tr into next tr; rep from * to end, working last tr into 3rd of ch 5, turn.

Row 7: Ch 5, sk first tr, 1 tr into next tr, * ch 4, 1 dtr into each of next 4 tr, ch 4, 1 tr into next tr, ch 2, 1 tr into next tr; rep from * to end, working last tr into 3rd of ch 5, turn.

Rep rows 2–7 for length required, ending with a row 6.

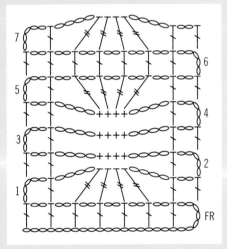

See page 50 for Stitch Key

SEASHORE TRELLIS

A combination of a trellis pattern and shell stitches, this stitch works well for a scarf or baby shawl. Choose a lightweight yarn to enhance the beauty of the stitch pattern.

Foundation chain: Work over a multiple of 12 stitches plus 3.

Foundation row: (RS) 2 tr into 4th ch from hook, * sk 2 chs, 1 dc into next ch, ch 5, sk 5 chs, 1 dc into next ch, sk 2 chs, 5 tr into next ch; rep from * to end, working only 3 tr into last ch, turn.

Row 1: Ch 1, 1 dc into first st, * ch 5, 1 dc into next ch 5 sp, ch 5, 1 dc into 3rd tr of next 5 tr group; rep from * to end, working last dc into 3rd of beg skipped ch 3, turn.

Row 2: * Ch 5, 1 dc into next ch 5 sp, 5 tr into next tr, 1 dc into next ch 5 sp; rep from * ending with ch 2, 1 tr into last dc, turn.

Row 3: Ch 1, 1 dc into first st, * ch 5, 1 dc into 3rd tr of next 5 tr group, ch 5, 1 dc into next ch 5 sp; rep from * to end, turn.

Row 4: Ch 3, 2 tr into first st, * 1 dc into next ch 5 sp, ch 5, 1 dc into next ch 5 sp, 5 tr into next dc; rep from * to end, working only 3 tr into last ch, turn.

Row 5: Ch 1, 1 dc into first st, * ch 5, 1 dc into next ch 5 sp, ch 5, 1 dc into 3rd tr of next 5 tr group; rep from * to end, working last dc into 3rd of beg skipped ch, turn.

Rep rows 2–5 for length required, ending with a row 4.

FAN LACE

This attractive, large-scale lace pattern is deceptively easy to work in double and treble crochet stitches. Work it in a soft cotton or cotton blend yarn to make a pretty wrap to wear on summer evenings.

Foundation chain: Work a multiple of 12 chains plus 3.

Foundation row: (RS) 1 tr into 4th ch from hook, 1 tr into each ch to end, turn.

Row 1: Ch 3, 2 tr into first tr, ch 2, sk next 3 tr, 1 dc into next tr, ch 5, sk next 3 tr, 1 dc into next tr, ch 2, sk next 3 tr, * 5 tr into next tr, ch 2, sk next 3 tr, 1 dc into next tr, ch 5, sk next 3 tr, 1 dc into next tr, ch 2, sk next 3 tr; rep from * ending with 3 tr into 3rd of beg skipped ch 3, turn.

Row 2: Ch 4, sk first tr, 1 tr into next tr, ch 1, 1 tr into next tr, ch 2, sk next ch 2 sp, 1 dc into next ch 5 sp, ch 2, * [1 tr into next tr, ch 1] 4 times, 1 tr into next tr, ch 2, sk next ch 2 sp, 1 dc into next ch 5 sp, ch 2; rep from * to last 2 tr, [1 tr into next tr, ch 1] twice, 1 tr into 3rd of ch 3, turn.

Row 3: Ch 5, sk first tr, 1 tr into next tr, ch 2, 1 tr into next tr, * sk next dc, [1 tr into next tr, ch 2] 4 times, 1 tr into next tr; rep from * to last dc, sk last dc, [1 tr into next tr, ch 2] twice, 1 tr into 3rd of ch 4, turn.

Row 4: Ch 3, 2 tr into next ch-2 sp, 1 tr into next tr, 2 tr into next ch 2 sp, sk next tr, 1 tr into next tr, * [2 tr into next ch 2 sp, 1 tr into next tr] 3 times, 2 tr into next ch 2 sp, sk next tr, 1 tr into next tr; rep from * to last ch 2 sp, 2 tr into last ch 2 sp, 1 tr into next tr, 2 tr into sp formed by ch 5, sk first 2 chs of ch 5, 1 tr into 3rd of ch 5, turn.

Row 5: Ch 3, 2 tr into first tr, ch 2, sk next 3 tr, 1 dc into next tr, ch 5, sk next 3 tr, 1 dc into next tr, ch 2, sk next 3 tr, * 5 tr into next tr, ch 2, sk next 3 tr, 1 dc into next tr, ch 5, sk next 3 tr, 1 dc into next tr, ch 2, sk next 3 tr; rep from * ending with 3 tr into 3rd of ch 3, turn.

Rep rows 2–5 for length required, ending with a row 4.

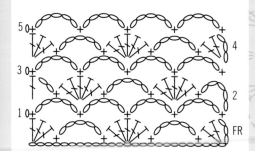

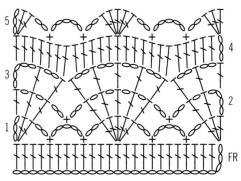

FILET CROCHET

Filet crochet is an openwork type of crochet characterized by a mesh background on which the pattern is picked out in solid blocks of stitches. It is traditionally worked in fine cotton thread, but also looks effective worked in yarn.

FILET CROCHET PATTERNS

Filet crochet patterns are always worked from a chart and these show the pattern as it will appear from the right side of the work. The chart rows are numbered at the sides, and you follow the numbered sequence, working upwards from the bottom of the chart (row 1) and from side to side (see diagram below).

A filet crochet "unit" comprises a beginning treble crochet, two chains for a space or two treble crochet stitches for a block and an ending treble crochet. The ending treble crochet stitch is also the beginning treble crochet of the next "unit".

Filet crochet charts begin with the first row, so the foundation chain is not shown. To calculate the number of stitches to make, you will need to multiply the number of squares across the chart by three and add one. For example, for a chart which is 20 squares across, make a foundation chain 61 chains long (20 x 3 + 1). You also need to add the correct number of turning chains, depending on whether the first chart row begins with a space or a block (see working the first row, right).

WORKING THE FIRST ROW

STARTING THE FIRST ROW WITH A SPACE

Make the foundation chain, calculating the number of chains as described above. Start to follow the chart from the bottom right-hand corner, along the row of squares marked 1. When the first square is a space, add four turning chains and work the first treble crochet stitch into the eighth chain from the hook. Continue working spaces and blocks along the row, reading the chart from right to left.

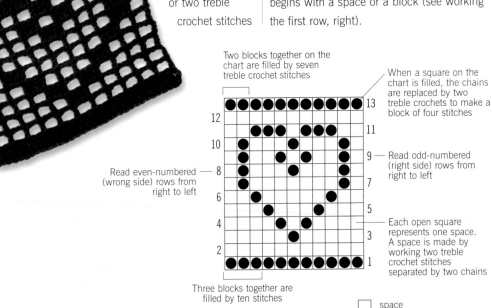

Two blocks together on the chart are filled by seven treble crochet stitches

When a square on the chart is filled, the chains are replaced by two treble crochets to make a block of four stitches

Read odd-numbered (right side) rows from right to left

Read even-numbered (wrong side) rows from right to left

Each open square represents one space. A space is made by working two treble crochet stitches separated by two chains

Three blocks together are filled by ten stitches

☐ space

⬤ block

See also: Openwork and Lace stitches, page 50

STARTING THE FIRST ROW WITH A BLOCK

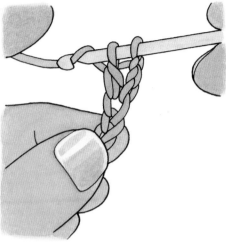

1 When the first square on the chart is a block, add two turning chains and work the first treble crochet stitch into the fourth chain from the hook.

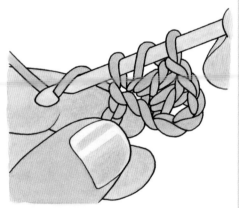

2 Work one treble crochet stitch into each of the next two chains to complete the first block. Continue along the row, reading the chart from right to left.

WORKING THE REST OF THE CHART ROWS

At the end of the first row, turn the work and follow the second row of the chart, reading from left to right. Work spaces and blocks at the beginning and end of the second and subsequent rows as follows.

WORKING A SPACE OVER A SPACE ON THE PREVIOUS ROW

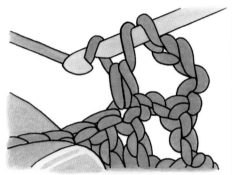

1 At the beginning of a row, work 5 turning chains (counts as 1 treble crochet stitch and 2 chains), skip the first stitch and the next 2 chains, work 1 treble crochet stitch into the next treble crochet stitch, then continue working the spaces and blocks from the chart.

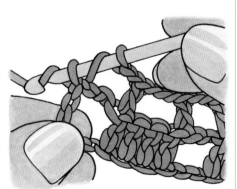

2 At the end of a row, finish with 1 treble crochet stitch into the last treble crochet stitch, work 2 chains, skip 2 chains, work 1 treble crochet stitch into the 3rd of 5 chains, turn.

WORKING A SPACE OVER A BLOCK ON THE PREVIOUS ROW

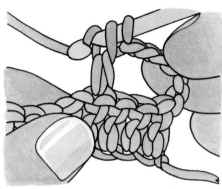

1 At the beginning of the row, work 5 turning chains (counts as 1 treble crochet stitch and 2 chains), skip the first 3 stitches, work 1 treble crochet stitch into the next treble crochet stitch, then continue working spaces and blocks from the chart.

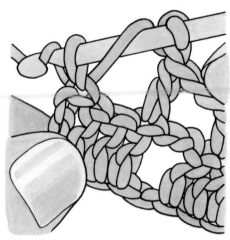

2 At the end of a row, work to the last 4 stitches. Work 1 treble crochet stitch into the next stitch, work 2 chains, skip 2 stitches, work 1 treble crochet stitch into the top of 3 chains to complete the block, turn.

WORKING A BLOCK OVER A SPACE ON THE PREVIOUS ROW

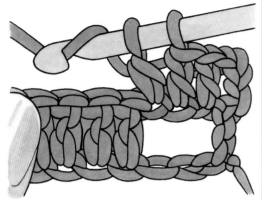

1 At the beginning of the row, work 3 turning chains (counts as 1 treble crochet stitch), skip 1 stitch, work 1 treble crochet stitch into each of the next 2 chains, 1 treble crochet stitch into the next stitch to complete the block. Continue across the row working spaces and blocks from the chart.

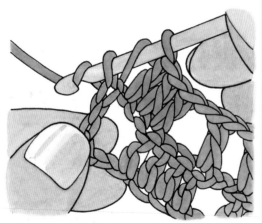

2 At the end of a row, finish with 1 treble crochet stitch into the last treble crochet stitch, 1 treble crochet stitch into each of the next 3 chains of the turning chain, turn.

WORKING A BLOCK OVER A BLOCK ON THE PREVIOUS ROW

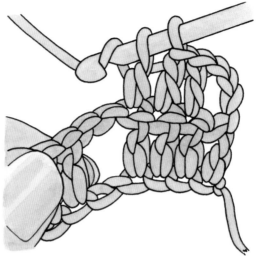

1 At the beginning of the row, work 3 turning chains (counts as 1 treble crochet stitch), skip 1 stitch, work 1 treble crochet stitch into each of the next 3 treble crochet stitches to complete the block. Continue across the row working spaces and blocks from the chart.

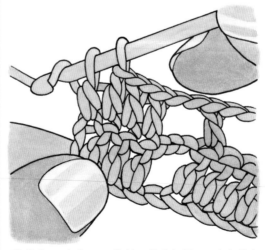

2 At the end of a row, finish with 1 treble crochet stitch into each of the last 3 treble crochet stitches, 1 treble crochet stitch into the top of 3 chains, turn.

STITCH
COLLECTION

STITCH KEY

Space ☐

Block

CHEQUER-BOARD

One of the simplest designs for filet crochet, this pattern is made by alternating blocks and spaces, and it is a great, easy-to-work stitch for making lightweight blankets and throws.

TINY FLOWERS

This design has a lighter feel than the chequer-board pattern. Groups of four blocks are arranged to make stylized flowers at regular intervals across the plain mesh background.

HEART

Filet crochet lends itself to working simplified motifs. In addition to working the heart motif, as shown in the chart, you can turn the chart on its side and work multiple repeats to make a lovely border.

SITTING CAT

This cat motif would look pretty repeated several times across the border of a baby shawl or snuggle blanket. Use a lightweight baby yarn and a fairly small hook to make the most of the design.

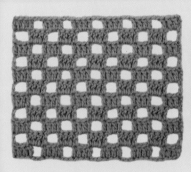

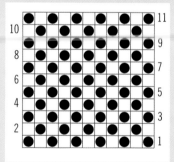

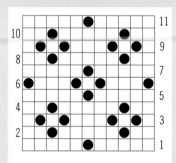

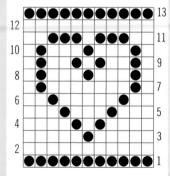

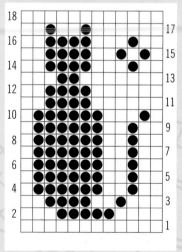

WORKING CHEVRON PATTERNS

Chevron patterns are worked in a similar way to plain horizontal stripes, but in this type of stripe pattern extra stitches are added and subtracted at regular intervals along each row.

The adding and subtracting of stitches forms a pattern of regular peaks and troughs, separated by blocks of stitches, and creates attractive patterns often known as ripple patterns. The peaks and troughs can form sharp points or gentle waves, depending on the pattern, and the effect can vary when the number of stitches in the blocks between the peaks and troughs is changed.

With basic chevron patterns, the pattern repeat is usually set on the first row after you have worked the foundation row of stitches into the foundation chain. This row is then repeated until the work is the required length. More complex chevron patterns, combining smooth, textured and lace stitches, are made up of peaks and troughs in a similar way, but each pattern repeat may take several rows to complete. Join new colours at the ends of the row in the same way as when working simple stripe patterns.

See also: **Basic Skills, page 12**
Working Stripe Patterns, page 32

WORKING A CHEVRON PATTERN IN DOUBLE CROCHET

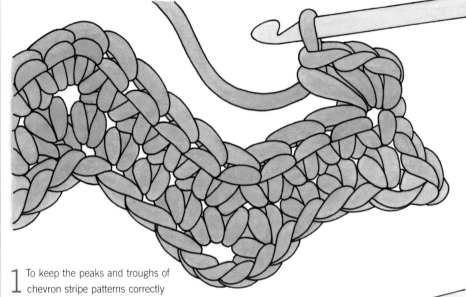

1 To keep the peaks and troughs of chevron stripe patterns correctly spaced, you may need to work one or more extra stitches at the beginning or end (or both) of every row. In this easy pattern, two double crochet stitches are worked into the first stitch of every row.

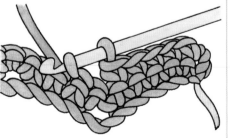

2 To make the bottom V-shapes of the chevron pattern (the troughs), skip two double crochet stitches (skip next 2 dc) at the bottom of the troughs, then continue working the next block of stitches.

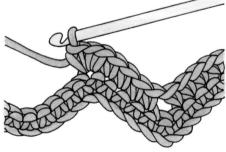

3 To make the top V-shapes of the chevrons (the peaks), work three double crochet stitches (3 dc into next dc) into the same stitch at the top of the peaks.

STITCH COLLECTION

DOUBLE CROCHET CHEVRONS

Yarn: Worked in three colours, A, B and C.

Foundation chain: Multiple of 11 chains plus 2.

Using yarn A, make the required length of foundation chain.

Foundation row: (RS) 2 dc into 2nd ch from hook, * 1 dc into each of next 4 chs, sk next 2 chs, 1 dc into each of next 4 chs, 3 dc into next ch; rep from * to end, ending last rep with 2 dc into last ch, turn.

Row 1: Ch 1, 2 dc into first dc, * 1 dc into each of next 4 dc, sk next 2 dc, 1 dc into each of next 4 dc, 3 dc into next dc; rep from * to end, ending last rep with 2 dc into last dc, turn.

Rep row 1, changing yarns in the following colour sequence:

4 rows in yarn A, 4 rows in yarn B, 4 rows in yarn C.

Repeat for length required.

Fasten off yarn.

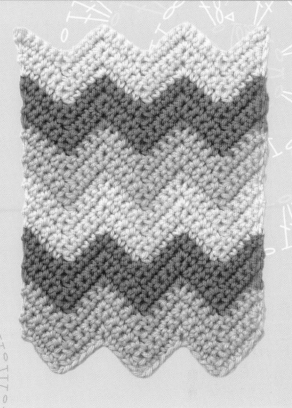

STITCH KEY

Foundation row	F R
Chain	o
Double crochet	+
Slip stitch	.
Treble crochet	┼
3 trebles together	

▸ Continued over the page

TREBLE CROCHET CHEVRONS

Yarn: Worked in two colours, A and B.

Foundation chain: Multiple of 13 chains.

Using yarn A, make the required length of foundation chain.

Foundation row: (RS) 1 tr into 4th ch from hook, 1 tr into each of next 3 chs, * 3 tr into next ch, 1 tr into each of next 5 chs, sk next 2 chs, 1 tr into each of next 5 chs; rep from * to last 6 chs, 3 tr into next ch, 1 tr into each of next 5 chs, turn,

Row 1: Sl st into 2nd tr, ch 3, 1 tr into each of next 4 tr, * 3 tr into next tr, 1 tr into each of next 5 tr, sk next 2 tr, 1 tr into each of next 5 tr; rep from * to last 6 sts, 3 tr into next tr, 1 tr into each of next 5 tr, turn.

Rep row 1, changing yarns in the following colour sequence:

2 rows in yarn A, 2 rows in yarn B.

Repeat for length required.

Fasten off yarn.

WAVY CHEVRONS

Yarn: Worked in three colours, A, B and C.

Foundation chain: Multiple of 14 chains plus 3.

Using yarn A, make the required length of foundation chain.

Foundation row: (RS) 2 tr into 4th ch from hook, 1 tr into each of next 3 chs, [tr3tog over next 3 chs] twice, 1 tr into each of next 3 chs, * 3 tr into each of next 2 chs, 1 tr into each of next 3 chs, [tr3tog over next 3 chs] twice, 1 tr into each of next 3 chs; rep from * to last ch, 3 tr into last ch, turn.

Row 1: Ch 3, 2 tr into first tr, 1 tr into each of next 3 tr, tr3tog twice, 1 tr into each of next 3 tr, * 3 tr into each of next 2 tr, 1 tr into each of next 3 tr, tr3tog twice, 1 tr into each of next 3 tr; rep from * to beg skipped chs, 3 tr into 3rd of beg skipped ch-3, turn.

Row 2: Ch 3, 2 tr into first tr, 1 tr into each of next 3 tr, tr3tog twice, 1 tr into each of next 3 tr, * 3 tr into each of next 2 tr, 1 tr into each of next 3 tr, tr3tog twice, 1 tr into each of next 3 tr; rep from * to turning ch, 3 tr into 3rd of ch-3, turn.

Rep row 2, changing yarns in the following colour sequence:

2 rows in yarn A, 1 row in yarn B, 2 rows in yarn A, 1 row in yarn C.

Repeat for length required.

Fasten off yarn.

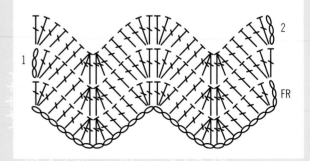

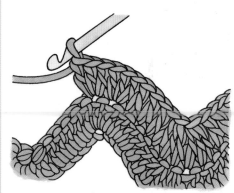

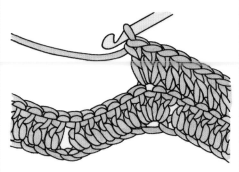

WORKING A CHEVRON PATTERN IN TREBLE CROCHET

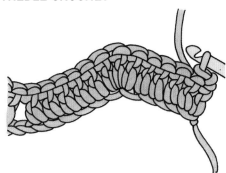

1 Instead of working extra stitches at the beginning of the row, you may be instructed to work one or more slip stitches in order to move the yarn and hook to the correct place for working the next row. In this pattern, turn and work a slip stitch into the second treble crochet of the row (sl st into 2nd tr) before working the turning chain.

2 Three stitches are worked into the same stitch of the previous row to form the "peaks". Work the block of stitches before the peak, then work three treble crochet stitches into the next treble crochet stitch (3 tr into next tr). The troughs are made in the same way as the double crochet pattern above, by simply skipping two stitches at the bottom of the troughs.

WORKING A WAVE PATTERN IN TREBLE CROCHET

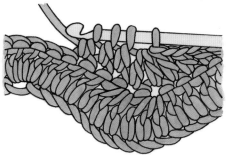

1 Soft waves are made by working two sets of increases and decreases into the peaks and troughs instead of one. To make the troughs, work three treble crochet stitches together (tr3tog) over the six stitches at the bottom of each trough.

2 To make the peaks, work three treble crochet stitches into each of the central two stitches at the top of the peaks (3 tr into each of next 2 tr).

See page 59 for Stitch Key

WORKING SPIKE STITCHES

Spike stitches (also called dropped stitches) are worked over the top of other stitches to add colour or texture to crochet. The stitches are worked singly or in groups over one or more rows and are usually worked in double crochet stitches.

As well as making interesting colour patterns, when worked in two or more contrasting colours, spike stitches also create a thick, densely worked fabric, without very much drape, which is good for making adult outerwear and accessories such as hats, purses and bags.

Spike stitches can be worked in any colour combination.

Spike stitches create a thick fabric.

TIP

When first trying out this technique, it's easier to see exactly what's happening if you work each row using a contrasting colour of yarn.

WORKING A BASIC DOUBLE CROCHET SPIKE STITCH

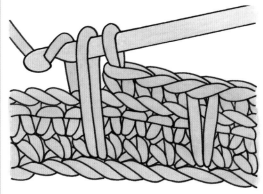

1 Insert the hook over the number of rows down from the row being worked as directed in the pattern instructions, taking the point right through the fabric to the wrong side. Wrap the yarn over the hook and draw through, lengthening the loop to the height of the working row.

2 To finish the spike, complete the stitch in the usual way. When working spike stitches, take care not to pull the loop too tight as this will distort the fabric.

STITCH COLLECTION

STITCH KEY

Foundation row	F R
Chain	o
Double crochet	+
Spike stitch	⌡
Join in new colour	◁

SPIKED STRIPES

Stripes of contrasting colours show off spike stitches to perfection. In this stitch, the colour changes after every two rows; with the colour not in use being carried loosely up the side to avoid lots of yarn ends.

Notes: SP = spike stitch made by inserting hook into work two rows below next stitch and working an dc.

Two contrasting yarn colours, A and B, are used to work this stitch.

Foundation chain: Using yarn A, work a multiple of 8 chains plus 1.

Foundation row: (RS) Using yarn A, 1 dc into 2nd ch from hook, 1 dc into each ch to end, turn.

Row 1: Using yarn A, ch 1, 1 dc into each dc to end, turn.

Join yarn B, but do not break yarn A.

Row 2: Using yarn B, ch 1, * 1 dc into each of next 3 dc, SP twice, 1 dc into each of next 3 dc; rep from * to end, turn.

Row 3: Using yarn B, ch 1, 1 dc into each dc to end, turn.

Row 4: Using yarn A, ch 1, 1 dc into each dc to end, turn.

Rep rows 1–4 for length required, ending with a row 1.

ALTERNATE SPIKES

This is a lovely stitch, which makes a thick, textured fabric. Worked in one colour, the fabric is reversible, so you can choose which side of the work you like best, and use that as the right side.

Notes: SP = spike stitch made by inserting hook into work one row below next stitch and working an dc.

Foundation chain: Work a multiple of 2 chains.

Foundation row: 1 dc into 2nd ch from hook, 1 dc into each ch to end, turn.

Row 1: Ch 1, 1 dc into first dc, * SP over next dc, 1 dc into next dc; rep from * to end, turn.

Row 2: Ch 1, 1 dc into each of first 2 dc, * SP over next dc, 1 dc into next dc; rep from * to last st, 1 dc into last dc, turn.

Rep row 2 for length required.

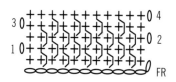

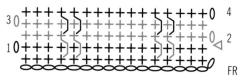

WORKING RAISED STITCHES

Stitches made with this technique are known by several different names: raised stitches, post stitches or relief stitches. They create a heavily textured surface, made by inserting the hook around the post (stem) of the stitches on the previous row, and then working a treble crochet stitch. The hook can be inserted from the front or the back of the work, giving a different effect each way.

INSERTING THE HOOK

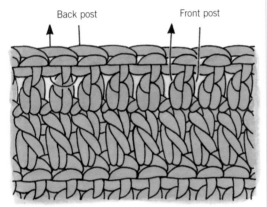

When working a front post stitch, insert the hook into the front of the fabric, round the back of the post, and return to the front of the work. When working a back post stitch, insert the hook from the back of the fabric, round the front of the post, and out through to the back of the work.

TIP

If you're finding it difficult to work out where to insert your hook, try practising this technique on a larger scale by using a thick yarn and large hook.

WORKING A RAISED STITCH FROM THE FRONT

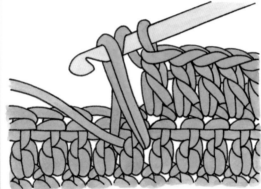

Wrap the yarn over the hook, insert the hook as described left, wrap the yarn again and draw up a loop on the front of the work. Complete the treble crochet stitch in the usual way.

WORKING A RAISED STITCH FROM THE BACK

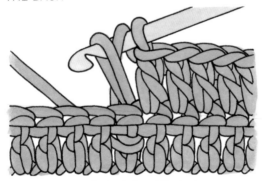

Wrap the yarn over the hook, insert the hook as described left, wrap the yarn again and draw up a loop at the back of the work. Complete the treble crochet stitch in the usual way.

STITCH COLLECTION

STITCH KEY

Foundation row	F R
Chain	○
Half treble crochet	⊤
Treble crochet	⅞
Raised treble crochet worked round front post	⅃
Raised treble crochet worked round back post	⅃

RAISED COLUMNS

Raised stitches look good when combined with other decorative crochet stitches, particularly those with a flatter surface. Here, vertical rows of raised stitches combine well with simple treble crochet shells.

Notes: FP = raised treble crochet stitch worked round the front post (front raised treble crochet stitch).

BP = raised treble crochet stitch worked round the back post (back raised treble crochet stitch).

Foundation chain: Work a multiple of 8 chains plus 2.

Foundation row: (RS) 2 tr into 6th ch from hook, * ch 2, 2 tr into next ch, sk next 2 chs, 1 htr into each of next 2 chs, sk next 2 chs, 2 tr into next ch; rep from * to last 3 chs, sk next 2 chs, 1 htr into last ch, turn.

Row 1: Ch 2, sk htr and next 2 tr, * [2 tr, ch 2, 2 tr] into next ch 2 sp, FP round each of next 2 htr; rep from * ending last rep with 1 tr into 5th of beg skipped ch 5, turn.

Row 2: Ch 2, sk first 3 tr, * [2 tr, ch 2, 2 tr] into next ch 2 sp, BP round each of next 2 tr; rep from * ending last rep with 1 tr into 2nd of ch 2, turn.

Row 3: Ch 2, sk first 3 tr, * [2 tr, ch 2, 2 tr] into next ch 2 sp, FP round each of next 2 tr; rep from * ending last rep with 1 tr into 2nd of ch 2, turn.

Rep rows 2 & 3 for length required, ending with a row 3.

BASKETWEAVE

This heavily worked stitch looks like a woven basket. It's perfect for making pillow covers and thick, warm throws and blankets, but you should remember that it will use up yarn very quickly.

Notes: FP = raised treble crochet stitch worked round the front post.

BP = raised treble crochet stitch worked round the back post.

Foundation chain: Work a multiple of 8 chains plus 4.

Foundation row: 1 tr into 4th ch from hook, 1 tr into each ch to end, turn.

Row 1: Ch 2, sk first tr, * FP round each of next 4 tr, BP round each of next 4 tr; rep from * ending last rep with 1 tr into 3rd of beg skipped ch 3, turn.

Rows 2, 3, 4: Ch 2, sk first tr, * FP round each of next 4 tr, BP round each of next 4 tr; rep from * ending last rep with 1 tr into 2nd of ch 2, turn.

Rows 5, 6, 7, 8: Ch 2, sk first tr, * BP round each of next 4 tr, FP round each of next 4 tr; rep from * ending last rep with 1 tr into 2nd of ch 2, turn.

Row 9: Ch 2, sk first tr, * FP round each of next 4 tr, BP round each of next 4 tr; rep from * ending last rep with 1 tr into 2nd of ch 2, turn.

Rep rows 2–9 for length required, ending with a row 4.

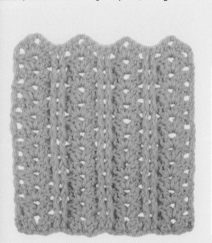

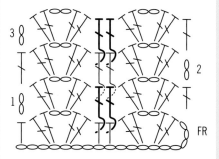

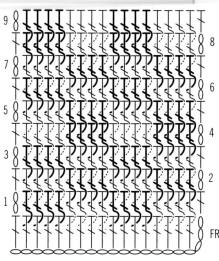

WORKING JACQUARD PATTERNS

Jacquard patterns are worked in two or more colours from a chart, usually in double crochet. This type of crochet creates a colourful, sturdy fabric, with a "woven" look to it.

Begin by working the foundation chain in the first colour. Calculate the number of chains to make according to the number of times you intend to repeat the pattern, then add one chain for turning. On the first row, work the first stitch into the second chain from the hook, then work the rest of the row in double crochet. Each square represents one stitch.

When changing yarns, carry the yarn not in use loosely across the back of the work and pick it up again when it is needed. This is called stranding and it works well when the areas of colour are narrow.

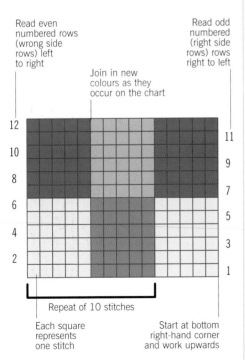

Read even numbered rows (wrong side rows) left to right

Read odd numbered (right side rows) rows right to left

Join in new colours as they occur on the chart

Repeat of 10 stitches

Each square represents one stitch

Start at bottom right-hand corner and work upwards

WORKING A TWO-COLOUR JACQUARD PATTERN

1 Make the required length of foundation yarn in yarn A, turn and begin to work the first row of the chart. When you reach the last stitch worked in yarn A, omit the last stage of the double crochet stitch, leaving two loops on the hook.

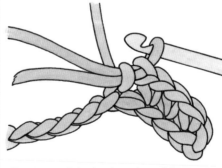

2 Join yarn B by drawing a loop of the new colour through the two loops on the hook. This completes the last double crochet stitch worked in yarn A. Don't break off yarn A.

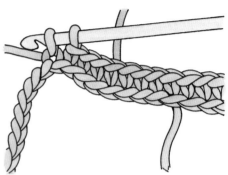

3 Continue to work across the chart in yarn B. When you reach the last stitch worked in yarn B, change back to yarn A by carrying it loosely behind the work. Draw a loop of it through to complete the colour change and finish the last stitch worked in yarn B. Continue changing yarns in the same way across the row, repeating the pattern as indicated on the chart.

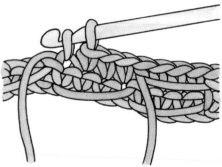

4 At the end of the row, turn and work the chart in the opposite direction from left to right. At the colour changes, bring the old colour forwards and take the new one to the back ready to complete the stitch partially worked in the old colour. Carry the colour not in use loosely along the wrong side of the work.

STITCH COLLECTION

JACQUARD STRIPES

Working several repeats of this simple two-row striped pattern makes a good practice piece. It's important to carry the yarn not in use loosely across the wrong side of the work to avoid it pulling and distorting the pattern.

JACQUARD CHECKS

This chequer-board pattern uses four different yarns, and looks best when four different shades of the same colour are used. Choose one light shade, one dark, and two slightly contrasting mid-tones.

KEY FOR JACQUARD STRIPES

yarn A

yarn B

KEY FOR JACQUARD CHECKS

yarn A

yarn B

yarn C

yarn D

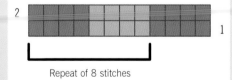

2

1

Repeat of 8 stitches

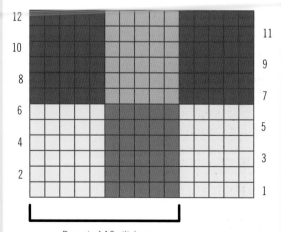

12

10

8

6

4

2

11

9

7

5

3

1

Repeat of 10 stitches

WORKING INTARSIA PATTERNS

Intarsia crochet produces a design that is visible on both sides of the fabric. Intarsia patterns are worked in two or more colours from a chart, in a similar way to jacquard patterns.

The main difference between intarsia and jacquard is that, in intarsia, the colour areas are larger and may be irregularly shaped, so colours not in use can't be carried across the back of the work. Instead, work each colour area using a separate ball of yarn.

Work the foundation chain in the first colour, working the same number of chains as the number of stitches across the chart, adding one chain for turning. If you're working a repeating intarsia pattern, calculate the number of chains to make in the same way as for a jacquard pattern.

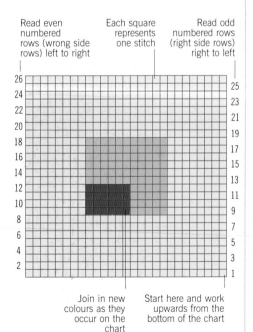

Read even numbered rows (wrong side rows) left to right

Each square represents one stitch

Read odd numbered rows (right side rows) right to left

26 24 22 20 18 16 14 12 10 8 6 4 2

25 23 21 19 17 15 13 11 9 7 5 3 1

Join in new colours as they occur on the chart

Start here and work upwards from the bottom of the chart

See also: **Working Jacquard Patterns, page 66**

WORKING AN INTARSIA PATTERN

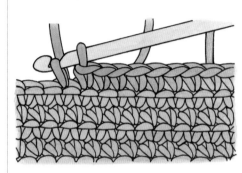

1 Make the required length of foundation yarn in yarn A, turn and work the plain rows at the bottom of the chart in double crochet. Work the first multicoloured row, beginning with yarn A. At the colour changes omit the last stage of the stitch before the change, leaving two loops on the hook. Join the next yarn by drawing a loop of the new colour through the two loops. This completes the last stitch worked in the first yarn. Continue in the same way along the row.

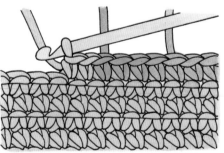

2 When you reach the last colour change in the row, where the chart indicates a change back to yarn A, work with another ball of the same yarn, not the one you used to begin the row.

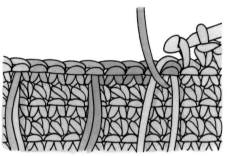

3 At the end of the row, turn and work from the chart in the opposite direction, from left to right. At each colour change, bring the old colour forwards and take the new one to the back ready to complete the stitch partially worked in the old colour, making sure that you loop the new yarn round the old one on the wrong side of the work to prevent holes.

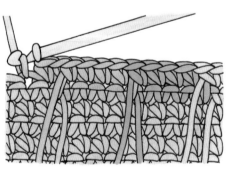

4 At the end of wrong side rows, make sure that all the yarns are back in the right place on the wrong side of the work.

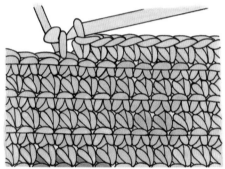

5 When you reach new areas of colour further up the chart, join in the yarns as before, making sure that you work each colour change into the last stitch of the previous colour.

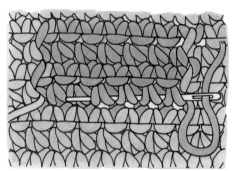

6 When you reach the point in the chart where all the stitches in a row are worked in yarn A, work across all the stitches using the original ball of this colour, working from right to left.

7 Take extra care when dealing with all the yarn ends on a piece of intarsia. Carefully darn each end into an area of crochet worked in the same colour so it won't be visible on the right side.

STITCH COLLECTION

INTARSIA BLOCKS

This simple block pattern will give you experience in working intarsia colour changes. You can work the chart exactly as it is, or repeat it several times to make a bigger piece of crochet.

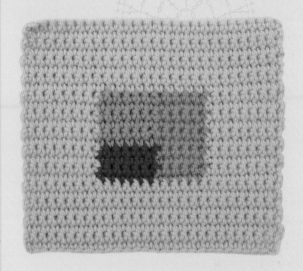

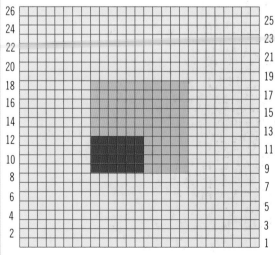

KEY

yarn A
yarn B
yarn C
yarn D

TUBULAR CROCHET

Tubular crochet is worked in the round using ordinary crochet hooks. Although the rounds are worked and joined in a similar way to those used to make a circular motif, the effect here is very different.

This type of crochet forms a cylinder, which can be as wide or narrow as you wish. This handy technique means that you can make an item such as a hat in one piece without a seam. Cylinders can also be combined with motifs or flat pieces of crochet to make garments and accessories.

Tubular crochet can be worked in three different ways, but each one begins with a length of chain joined into a ring. You can work rounds of double crochet stitches without making a join; this forms a spiral shape. When using taller stitches such as treble crochet, each round is joined to make a seam. If you turn the work at the end of each round, you'll produce a straight seam; if you continue working in the same direction on every round, the seam will gradually spiral round the cylinder.

Double crochet cylinder worked in a spiral.

Treble crochet cylinder worked with turns.

Treble crochet cylinder worked without turns.

See also: **Working Circular Motifs, page 72**

WORKING A SPIRAL CYLINDER IN DOUBLE CROCHET

1 Make the required length of chain and join it into a ring with a slip stitch. Turn and work one row of double crochet into the chain. Join the round by working a double crochet into the first stitch.

2 Insert a split ring marker into the double crochet just worked to mark the beginning of a new round. Continue the new round, working a double crochet into each stitch of the previous round.

3 When you reach the marker, don't join the round. Instead, remove the marker and work the marked stitch.

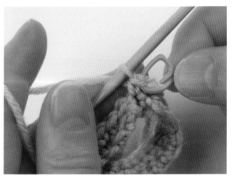

4 Replace the marker in the new stitch to mark the start of the new round. Continue working round and round, moving the marker each time you reach it, until the cylinder is the required length, then fasten off the yarn.

WORKING A TREBLE CROCHET CYLINDER WITHOUT TURNS

1 Make the required length of chain and join it into a ring with a slip stitch.

2 Work three chains (or the correct number of chains for the stitch you are using) to start the first round.

3 Work one treble crochet stitch into each chain until you reach the end of the round.

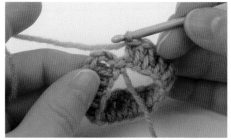

4 Join the first round by working a slip stitch into the third of the three turning chains.

5 Continue to work the next and subsequent rounds in treble crochet, joining each round with a slip stitch as before. When all the rounds have been worked, fasten off the yarn.

WORKING A TREBLE CROCHET CYLINDER WITH TURNS

1 Work the foundation chain and first round of stitches as for step 1, above. Join with a slip stitch and work three chains.

2 Turn the cylinder to reverse the direction and work three chains to begin the next round. You will be working this round from the inside of the cylinder.

3 Work one treble crochet stitch into each stitch until you reach the end of the round.

4 Join the round by working a slip stitch into the third of the three turning chains. Turn and work three chains, then work the next round from the outside of the cylinder. Repeat from step 2, making sure you turn the work at the beginning of every round.

WORKING CIRCULAR MOTIFS

Working crochet in flat rounds rather than backwards and forwards in straight rows offers a new range of possibilities to make colourful and intricate pieces of crochet called motifs or medallions.

Crochet motifs are worked outwards from a central ring and the number of stitches on each round increases. Evenly spaced increases result in a flat, circular motif, but when the increases are grouped together to make corners, the resulting motif can be a square, hexagon or other flat shape. Motifs can be solid, textured or lacy in appearance. They are joined together using a variety of techniques to make afghans, shawls and wraps, as well as simply shaped garments.

WORKING IN ROUNDS

The usual way of starting to work a motif is to make a short length of chain and join it into a ring. The ring can be made any size, depending on the pattern instructions, and can leave a small or large hole at the centre of the motif.

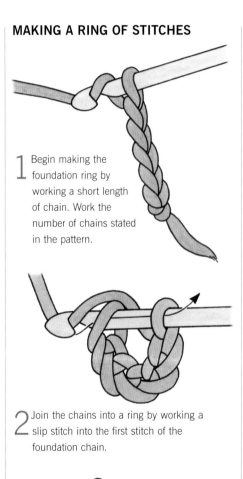

See also: **Basic Skills, page 12**
Joining Yarns, page 22

MAKING A RING OF STITCHES

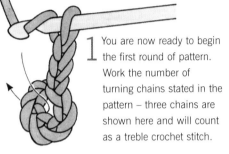

1 Begin making the foundation ring by working a short length of chain. Work the number of chains stated in the pattern.

2 Join the chains into a ring by working a slip stitch into the first stitch of the foundation chain.

3 Gently tighten the first stitch by pulling the loose yarn end with your left hand. The foundation ring is now complete.

WORKING INTO THE RING

1 You are now ready to begin the first round of pattern. Work the number of turning chains stated in the pattern – three chains are shown here and will count as a treble crochet stitch.

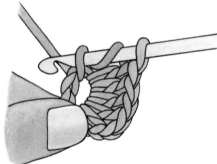

2 Inserting the hook into the space at the centre of the ring each time, work the correct number of stitches into the ring as stated in the pattern. Count the stitches at the end of the round to make sure you have worked the correct number.

3 Join the first and last stitches of the round together by working a slip stitch into the top of the turning chain.

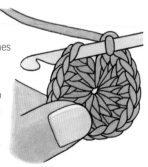

MAKING A YARN RING

This alternative method of making a foundation ring is useful as the yarn end is enclosed in the first round of stitches and will not need weaving in later. It should not be used with slippery yarns such as mercerized cotton or silk blends because the yarn end may work loose.

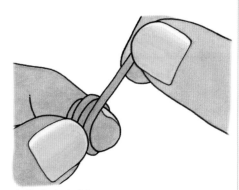

1 Begin by holding the yarn end between the thumb and first finger of your left hand and wind the yarn several times round the tip of your finger.

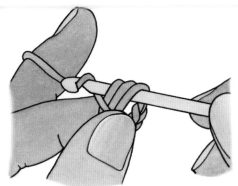

2 Carefully slip the yarn ring off your finger. Inserting the hook into the ring, pull a loop of yarn through and work a double crochet stitch to secure the ring. Work the specified number of turning chains and the first round of pattern into the ring in the usual way.

FASTENING OFF

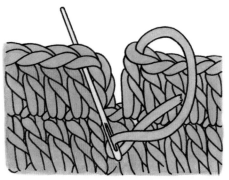

1 For a really neat edge on the final round, use this method of sewing the first and last stitches together in preference to the slip stitch method shown above. Cut the yarn, leaving an end of about 10 cm (4 in), and draw it through the last stitch. With right side facing, thread the end into a large yarn needle and take it under both loops of the stitch next to the turning chain.

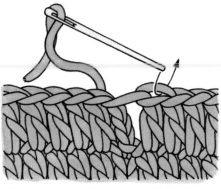

2 Pull the needle through, insert it into the centre of the last stitch of the round. On the wrong side, pull the needle through to complete the stitch, adjust the length of the stitch to close the round, then weave in the end on the wrong side in the usual way.

JOINING CIRCULAR MOTIFS

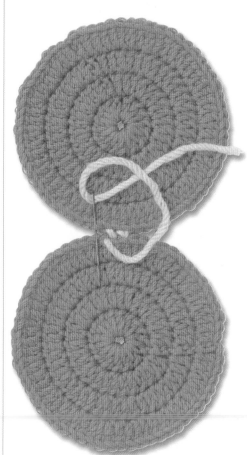

Circular motifs are often worked in a variety of yarns and sizes to make items such as coasters and table mats. They join less easily than motifs with straight sides because of their curved shape, and look best arranged in rows and sewn together with a few stitches where the curves touch.

STITCH COLLECTION

CIRCLE WITH SPOKES

Yarn: Worked in one colour.

Foundation ring: Ch 6 and join with sl st to form a ring.

Round 1: Ch 5 (counts as 1 tr, ch 2), [1 tr, ch 2] into ring 7 times, join with sl st into 3rd of ch 5. (8 spaced tr).

Round 2: Ch 3 (counts as 1 tr), 2 tr into same place, ch 2, [3 tr into next tr, ch 2] 7 times, join with sl st into 3rd of ch 3.

Round 3: Ch 3 (counts as 1 tr), 1 tr into same place, 1 tr into next tr, 2 tr into next tr, ch 2, [2 tr into next tr, 1 tr into next tr, 2 tr into next tr, ch 2] 7 times, join with sl st into 3rd of ch 3.

Round 4: Ch 1, 1 dc into each tr of previous round, working 2 dc into each ch 2 sp, join with sl st into first dc.

Fasten off yarn.

STITCH KEY

Chain	
Slip stitch	•
Double crochet	+
Treble crochet	
Beginning cluster	
Cluster made from 3 trebles	
Beginning cluster made from 3 trebles	
Cluster made from 4 trebles	
Fasten off	
Join in	

TREBLE CROCHET CIRCLE

Yarn: Worked in one colour.

Foundation ring: Ch 6 and join with sl st to form a ring.

Round 1: Ch 3 (counts as 1 tr), 15 tr into ring, join with sl st into 3rd of ch 3. (16 tr).

Round 2: Ch 3 (counts as 1 tr), 1 tr into same place, 2 tr into each st of previous round, join with sl st into 3rd of ch 3. (32 tr).

Round 3: Ch 3 (counts as 1 tr), 1 tr into same place, *[1 tr into next st, 2 tr into next st]; rep from * to last st, 1 tr into last st, join with sl st into 3rd of ch 3. (48 tr).

Round 4: Ch 3 (counts as 1 tr), 1 tr into same place, *[1 tr into each of next 2 sts, 2 tr into next st]; rep from * to last 2 sts, 1 tr into each of last 2 sts, join with sl st into 3rd of ch 3. (64 tr).

Fasten off yarn.

This circle can be made larger than shown by working one more treble crochet stitch between the increases on each subsequent round.

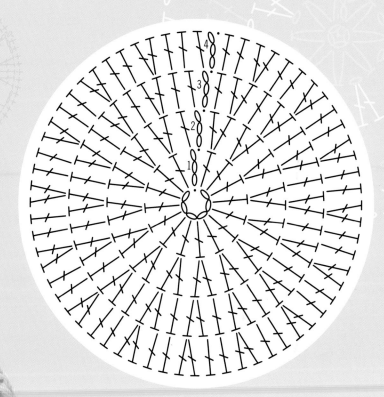

STRIPED TREBLE CROCHET CIRCLE

Work this motif using the same pattern as an ordinary treble crochet circle, but change the yarn colour every round. Leave a yarn tail of about 10 cm (4 in) at each colour change and weave the ends in on the wrong side when the circle is complete.

▶ **Continued over the page**

SUNBURST CIRCLE

Yarn: Worked in three colours, A, B and C.

Special abbreviations: Beg cl = beginning cluster made from 2 tr sts, cl = cluster made from 3 tr sts.

Foundation ring: Using yarn A, ch 4 and join with sl st to form a ring.

Round 1: Ch 1, 6 dc into ring, join with sl st into first dc.

Round 2: Ch 1, 2 dc into next dc 6 times, join with sl st into first dc. (12 dc).

Round 3: Ch 1, 2 dc into next dc 12 times, join with sl st into first dc. (24 dc). Break off yarn A.

Round 4: Join yarn B to any dc, ch 3 (counts as 1 tr), beg cl into same dc, ch 2, miss next dc, * cl into next dc, ch 2, miss next dc; rep from * 10 times, join with sl st into top of beg cl. Break off yarn B.

Round 5: Join yarn C to any ch 2 sp, ch 3 (counts as 1 tr), beg cl into same sp, ch 3, * cl into next ch 2 sp, ch 3; rep from * 10 times, join with sl st into top of beg cl.

Round 6: Ch 3, 2 tr into top of beg cl, 3 tr into next ch 3 sp, *3 tr into top of next cl, 3 tr into next ch 3 sp; rep from * 10 times, join with sl st into 3rd of ch 3.

Fasten off yarn.

See page 74 for Stitch Key

CLUSTER CIRCLE

Yarn: Worked in one colour.

Special abbreviations: Beg cl = beginning cluster made from 3 tr sts, cl = cluster made from 4 tr sts.

Foundation ring: Using yarn A, ch 6 and join with sl st to form a ring.

Round 1: Ch 1, 12 dc into ring, join with sl st into first dc.

Round 2: Ch 4 (counts as 1 tr, ch 1), * 1 tr into next dc, ch 1; rep from * 10 times, join with sl st into 3rd of ch 4. (12 spaced tr.)

Round 3: Sl st into next ch 1 sp, ch 3 (counts as 1 tr), beg cl into same sp, ch 3, * cl into next ch 1 sp, ch 3; rep from * 10 times, join with sl st into top of beg cl. (12 clusters).

Round 4: Sl st into next ch 3 sp, ch 3 (counts as 1 tr), beg cl into same sp, * ch 2, 1 tr into top of next cl, ch 2, ** cl into next ch 3 sp; rep from * 10 times and from * to ** once again, join with sl st into top of beg cl.

Round 5: Ch 1, 3 dc into each ch 2 sp of previous round, join with sl st into first dc.

Fasten off yarn.

WORKING AND JOINING SQUARES

Square motifs are worked in a similar way to circular motifs, starting at the centre with a foundation chain and working outwards in rounds.

Extra stitches or chains are worked at regular intervals on some of the rounds to form corners. Some motifs (Granny square) begin with a small circle at the centre, while others (Circle in a square) have several rounds worked before the corners are made.

JOINING SQUARE MOTIFS

Square motifs can be stitched together or joined with rows of slip stitches or double crochet. For the neatest join, work the stitches through the back loops of the crochet. To make a stronger, but more visible join, work the stitches through both loops.

JOINING MOTIFS WITH STITCHING

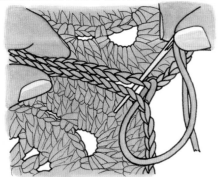

1 Lay the motifs out in the correct order with the right sides up. Working in horizontal rows, stitch the motifs together, beginning with the top row of motifs. Begin stitching at the right-hand edge of the first two motifs, sewing into the back loop of corresponding stitches.

See also: **Basic Skills, page 12**
Working Circular Motifs, page 72

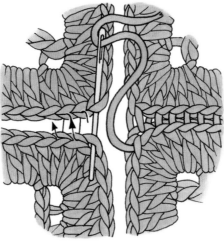

2 Continue stitching the first two motifs together, making sure you join only the back loops of each edge together, until you reach the left-hand corner. Align the next two motifs, carry the yarn firmly across and join them together in the same way. For extra strength, you can work two stitches into the corner loops before and after carrying the yarn across. Continue joining motifs along the row, then secure the yarn ends carefully at the beginning and end of the stitching. Repeat until all the horizontal edges of the motifs are joined.

3 Turn the crochet so the unstitched edges of the motifs are now horizontal. Working in the same way as above, join the remaining edges together with horizontal rows of stitching. When working the corners, take the needle under the stitch made on the previous row.

TIP

When joining two differently coloured squares by stitching them together, use a yarn that matches one of the squares so the stitches are less noticeable.

JOINING MOTIFS WITH SLIP STITCH

Joining motif edges by slip stitching them together with a crochet hook makes a firm seam with an attractive ridge on the right side. To add interest, use a contrasting yarn colour to work the slip stitch rows.

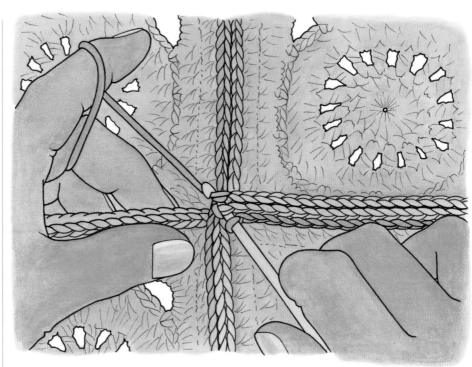

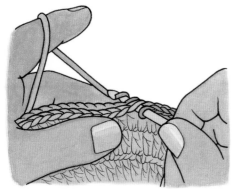

1 Lay the motifs out as above and work all the horizontal seams first. Place the first two motifs together, wrong sides facing, and work a row of slip stitch through both loops of each motif.

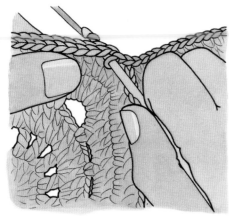

2 When you reach the corner, align the next two motifs, carry the yarn firmly across and join them together in the same way. Continue joining motifs along the row in the same way, keeping your tension even. Secure the yarn ends carefully, then repeat until all the horizontal edges of the motifs are joined.

3 Turn the work so the remaining edges of the motifs are now horizontal. Working in the same way as above, join the remaining edges together with horizontal rows of slip stitch. When working the corners, carry the yarn firmly across the ridge.

TIP

If you're finding it difficult inserting your hook through the edges of the squares, use a slightly smaller hook or one which has a more pointed tip.

JOINING WITH DOUBLE CROCHET

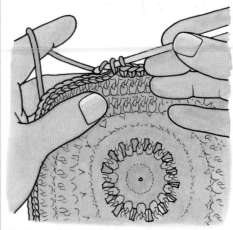

Double crochet can also be used to join edges together, and it makes a strong but rather bulky and thick seam. Work as for slip stitch joins above, but place the motifs right sides together and work rows of double crochet through both loops of the crochet edge.

STITCH COLLECTION

STITCH KEY

Chain	⬭
Double crochet	+
Slip stitch	•
Treble crochet	┬
Double treble crochet	‡
Beginning cluster made from 2 trebles	⫚
Cluster made from 3 trebles	⬥
Fasten off	◀
Join in	◁

CROYDON SQUARE

Yarn: Worked in three colours, A, B and C.

Special abbreviations: beg cl = beginning cluster made from 2 tr sts, cl = cluster made from 3 tr sts.

Foundation ring: Using yarn A, ch 4 and join with sl st to form a ring.

Round 1: Ch 4 (counts as 1 tr, ch 1), [1 tr into ring, ch 1] 11 times, join with sl st into 3rd of ch 4. (12 spaced tr).

Round 2: Ch 3 (counts as 1 tr), beg cl in same sp, [ch 3, cl into next ch, 1 sp] 11 times, ch 3, join with sl st into top of beg cl.

Round 3: Sl st into centre st of next ch 3 sp, ch 1, 1 dc into same sp, [ch 5, 1 dc into next ch 3 sp] 11 times, join with sl st into first dc. Break off yarn A.

Round 4: Join yarn B to centre st of any ch 5 sp, ch 3 (counts as 1 tr), 4 tr into same sp, * ch 1, 1 dc into next ch 5 sp, ch 5, 1 dc into next ch 5 sp, ch 1, ** [5 tr, ch 3, 5 tr] into next ch 5 sp; rep from * twice and from * to ** once again, 5 tr into next ch 5 sp, ch 3, join with sl st into 3rd of ch 3. Break off yarn B.

Round 5: Join yarn C to any ch 3 sp, ch 3 (counts as 1 tr), [1 tr, ch 2, 2 tr] into same sp, * 1 tr into each of next 4 tr, ch 4, 1 dc into next ch 5 sp, ch 4, miss next tr, 1 tr into each of next 4 tr, ** [2 tr, ch 2, 2 tr] into next ch 3 sp; rep from * twice and from * to ** once again, join with sl st into 3rd of ch 3.

Round 6: Sl st in next tr and into next ch 2 sp, ch 3 (counts as 1 tr), [1 tr, ch 2, 2 tr] into same sp, * 1 tr into each of next 4 tr, [ch 4, 1 dc into next ch 4 sp] twice, ch 4, sk next 2 tr, 1 tr into each of next 4 tr, ** [2 tr, ch 2, 2 tr] into next ch 2 sp; rep from * twice and from * to ** once again, join with sl st into 3rd of ch 3.

Round 7: Ch 1, 1 dc into same place, 1 dc into each tr of previous round, working 4 dc into each ch 4 sp along sides and 3 dc into each ch 2 corner sp, join with sl st into first dc.

Fasten off yarn.

CIRCLE IN A SQUARE

Yarn: Worked in one colour.

Foundation ring: Ch 6 and join with sl st to form a ring.

Round 1: Ch 3 (counts as 1 tr), work 15 tr into ring, join with sl st to 3rd of ch 3 (16 tr).

Round 2: Ch 5 (counts as 1 tr, ch 2), [1 tr into next tr, ch 2] 15 times, join with sl st into 3rd of ch 5.

Round 3: Ch 3, 2 tr into ch 2 sp, ch 1, [3 tr, ch 1] into each ch 2 sp, join with sl st into 3rd of ch 3.

Round 4: * [ch 3, 1 dc into next sp] 3 times, ch 6 (corner sp made), 1 dc into next ch 1 sp; rep from * to end, join with sl st into first of ch 3.

Round 5: Ch 3, 2 tr into first ch 3 sp, 3 tr into each of next two ch 3 sps, * [5 tr, ch 2, 5 tr] into corner sp, 3 tr into each ch 3 sp; rep from * to end, join with sl st into 3rd of ch 3.

Round 6: Ch 3, 1 tr into each tr of previous round, working [1 tr, 1 dtr, 1 tr] into each ch 2 corner sp, join with sl st into 3rd of ch 3.

Fasten off yarn.

▸ **Continued over the page**

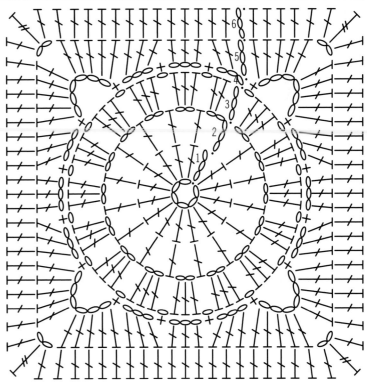

GRANNY SQUARE

Yarn: Worked in four colours, A, B, C and D.

Foundation ring: Using yarn A, ch 6 and join with sl st to form a ring.

Round 1: Ch 3 (counts as 1 tr), 2 tr into ring, ch 3, * 3 tr into ring, ch 3; rep from * twice more, join with sl st into 3rd of ch 3. Break off yarn A.

Round 2: Join yarn B to any ch 3 sp, ch 3 (counts as 1 tr), [2 tr, ch 3, 3 tr] into same sp (corner made), * ch 1, [3 tr, ch 3, 3 tr] into next ch 3 sp; rep from * twice more, ch 1, join with sl st into 3rd of ch 3. Break off yarn B.

Round 3: Join yarn C to any ch 3 corner sp, ch 3 (counts as 1 tr), [2 tr, ch 3, 3 tr] into same sp, * ch 1, 3 tr into ch 1 sp, ch 1, ** [3 tr, ch 3, 3 tr] into next ch 3 corner sp; rep from * twice and from * to ** once again, join with sl st into 3rd of ch 3. Break off yarn C.

Round 4: Join yarn D to any ch 3 corner sp, ch 3 (counts as 1 tr), [2 tr, ch 3, 3 tr] into same sp, * [ch 1, 3 tr] into each ch 1 sp along side of square, ch 1, **[3 tr, ch 3, 3 tr] into next ch 3 corner sp; rep from * twice and from * to ** once again, join with sl st into 3rd of ch 3. Break off yarn D.

Round 5: Join yarn A to any ch 3 corner sp, ch 3 (counts as 1 tr), [2 tr, ch 3, 3 tr] into same sp, * [ch 1, 3 tr] into each ch 1 sp along side of square, ch 1, ** [3 tr, ch 3, 3 tr] into next ch 3 corner sp; rep from *.

Round 6: Sl st into next ch 3 corner sp, ch 3 (counts as 1 tr), [2 tr, ch 3, 3 tr] into same sp, * [ch 1, 3 tr] into each ch 1 sp along side of square, ch 1, ** [3 tr, ch 3, 3 tr] into next ch 3 corner sp; rep from * twice and from * to ** once again, join with sl st into 3rd of ch 3.

Fasten off yarn.

See page 80 for Stitch Key

WORKING AND JOINING HEXAGONS

Hexagonal motifs are worked in a similar way to circular and square motifs, but they need different sequences of increases to make six corners. Hexagonal motifs with a solidly crocheted last round can be stitched or crocheted together to make large pieces of crochet such as afghans, throws and shawls in the same way as square motifs.

You can join hexagons into long strips and then join the strips together, or simply lay the pieces out in the required arrangement and join the edges that touch with separate seams. Pay special attention to securing the yarn ends neatly at the beginning and end of each seam.

When joining motifs such as the Classic hexagon which have a lacy last round, you can crochet these together as you work.

WORKING HEXAGONS

The centres of hexagonal motifs may have a circular or hexagonal shape, depending on the pattern. When working a motif with a hexagonal centre, remember that you'll be working six corners rather than four needed for a square, so you need to work the foundation ring fairly loosely to ensure that the finished hexagon will lie flat.

See also: **Basic Skills, page 12**
Working Circular Motifs, page 72
Working and Joining Squares, page 78

BEGINNING WITH A HEXAGON SHAPE

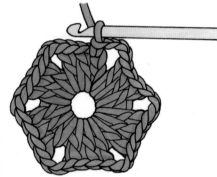

1 Work the foundation ring, then work six groups of stitches separated by chain spaces as indicated in the pattern to make a hexagon shape. Join the round with a slip stitch in the usual way.

2 On the second round, work two groups of stitches separated by a chain space into each of the chain spaces on the previous round to continue making a hexagon shape. Work further rows as indicated in the pattern.

BEGINNING WITH A CIRCLE

1 Work the foundation ring, then work the number of stitches indicated in the pattern. The stitches form a circle and they may be solidly worked or separated by a single chain space. Join the round with a slip stitch in the usual way.

2 On the second round, work groups of stitches separated by chain spaces into the previous round. This creates a hexagon shape in which the corners are formed by chain spaces rather than by groups of stitches. The chain spaces act as a foundation for corners worked on the next and subsequent rounds.

JOINING HEXAGONS AS YOU WORK

To begin, work one complete motif, then join the edges of further motifs to the original one as you work the final rounds. You can join the first few hexagons to make a strip and use this as a base for attaching the remaining motifs if you're making a rectangular piece, or simply begin with one motif and let your piece grow outwards from the centre.

2 Return to the second hexagon and work a treble crochet stitch into it to complete the corner.

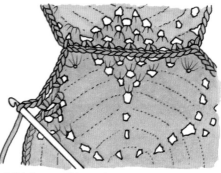

4 Work one treble crochet to complete the corner, then work the remainder of the last round as given in the pattern. Fasten off the yarn.

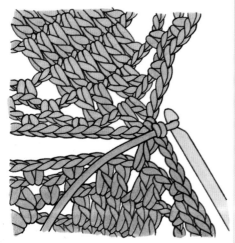

1 Work the second motif until you reach the last round. Work in pattern along the first side, then work the first treble crochet of the corner group. Align the edges of both hexagons and join by working a double crochet into the chain space of the corner on the first hexagon.

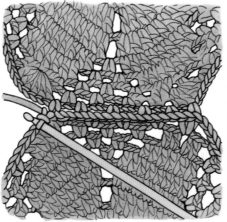

3 Continue working round the second hexagon, joining the chain spaces of each hexagon together by working one chain, one double crochet into the opposite chain space, one chain until you reach the next corner. At the corner, work the first treble crochet of the pattern, one double crochet into the chain space of the first hexagon.

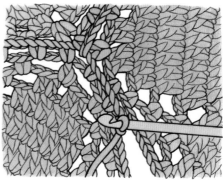

5 Join further hexagons to the first two in the same way, joining one, two or more edges as required.

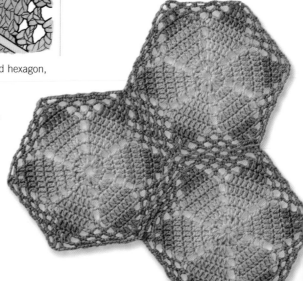

STITCH COLLECTION

STITCH KEY

Chain	⊙
Slip stitch	•
Double crochet	+
Treble crochet	╪
Double treble crochet	╪╪
Join new colour	◀
Fasten off	◁

CLASSIC HEXAGON

Yarn: Worked in three colours, A, B and C.

Foundation ring: Using yarn A, ch 6 and join with sl st to form a ring.

Round 1: Ch 4 (counts as 1 tr, ch 1), [1 tr into ring, ch 1] 11 times, join with sl st into 3rd of ch 4. (12 spaced tr).

Round 2: Ch 3 (counts as 1 tr), 2 tr into next ch 1 sp, 1 tr into next tr, ch 2, * 1 tr into next tr, 2 tr into next ch 1 sp, 1 tr into next tr, ch 2; rep from * 4 times, join with sl st to 3rd of ch 3.

Round 3: Ch 3, 1 tr into same place, 1 tr into each of next 2 tr, 2 tr into next tr, ch 2, * 2 tr into next tr, 1 tr into each of next 2 tr, 2 tr into next tr, ch 2; rep from * 4 times, join with sl st to 3rd of ch 3. Break off yarn A.

Round 4: Join yarn B. Ch 3, 1 tr into same place, 1 tr into each of next 4 tr, 2 tr into next tr, ch 2, * 2 tr into next tr, 1 tr into each of next 4 tr, 2 tr into next tr, ch 2; rep from * 4 times, join with sl st to 3rd of ch 3.

Round 5: Ch 3, 1 tr into each of next 7 tr, * ch 3, 1 dc into next ch 2 sp, ch 3, 1 tr into each of next 8 tr; rep from * 4 times, ch 3, 1 dc into next ch 2 sp, ch 3, join with sl st to 3rd of ch 3. Break off yarn B.

Round 6: Join yarn C. Sl st into next tr, ch 3, 1 tr into each of next 5 tr, * ch 3, [1 dc into next ch 3 sp, ch 3] twice, skip next tr, 1 tr into each of next 6 tr; rep from * 4 times, ch 3, [1 dc into next ch 3 sp, ch 3] twice, join with sl st to 3rd of ch 3.

Round 7: Sl st into next tr, ch 3, 1 tr into each of next 3 tr, ch 3, * [1 dc into next ch 3 sp, ch 3] 3 times, skip next tr, 1 tr into each of next 4 tr; rep from * 4 times, ch 3, [1 dc into next ch 3 sp, ch 3] 3 times, join with sl st to 3rd of ch 3.

Round 8: Sl st between 2nd and 3rd tr of group, ch 4 (counts as 1 tr, ch 1), 1 tr into same place, * ch 3, [1 dc into next ch 3 sp, ch 3] 4 times, [1 tr, ch 1, 1 tr] between 2nd and 3rd tr of group; rep from * 4 times, ch 3, [1 dc into ch 3 sp, ch 3] 4 times, join with sl st to 3rd of ch 4.

Fasten off yarn.

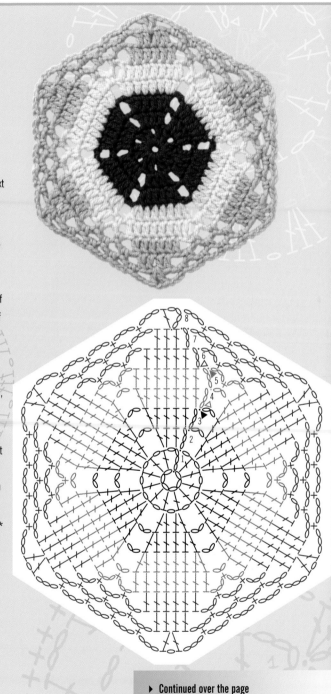

▶ **Continued over the page**

WHEEL HEXAGON

Yarn: Worked in one colour.

Foundation ring: Ch 6 and join with sl st to form a ring.

Round 1: Ch 6 (counts as 1 dtr, ch 2), 1 dtr into ring, * ch 2, 1 dtr into ring; rep from * 9 times, ch 2, join with sl st into 4th of ch 6. (12 spaced dtr).

Round 2: Sl st into next ch 2 sp, ch 3 (counts as 1 tr), [1 tr, ch 2, 2 tr] into same ch 2 sp as sl st, * 3 tr into next ch 2 sp, [2 tr, ch 2, 2 tr] into next ch 2 sp; rep from * 4 times, 3 tr into next ch 2 sp, join with sl st into 3rd of ch 3.

Round 3: Ch 3 (counts as 1 tr), 1 tr into next tr, [2 tr, ch 3, 2 tr] into next ch 2 sp, 1 tr into each of next 7 tr, * [2 tr, ch 3, 2 tr] into next ch 2 sp, 1 tr into each of next 7 tr; rep from * 4 times, ending last rep.

Round 4: Ch 3 (counts as 1 tr), 1 tr into each of next 3 tr, * 3 tr into next ch 3 sp, 1 tr into each of next 11 tr; rep from * 4 times, 3 tr into next ch 3 sp, 1 tr into each of next 7 tr, join with sl st into 3rd of ch 3.

Fasten off yarn.

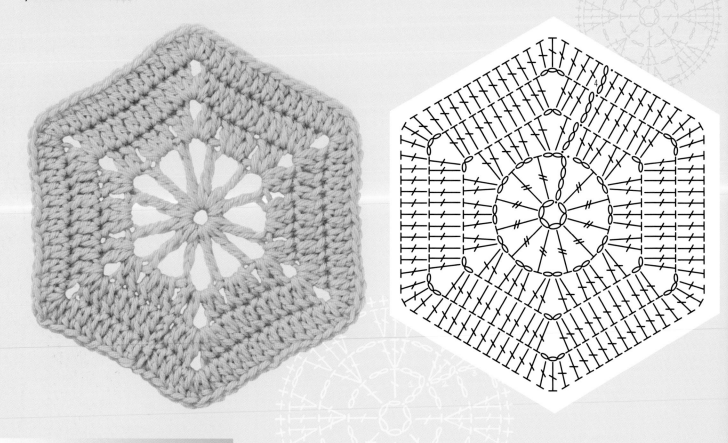

See page 85 for Stitch Key

GRANNY HEXAGON

Yarn: Worked in three colours, A, B and C.

Foundation ring: Using yarn A, ch 8 and join with sl st to form a ring.

Round 1: Ch 3 (counts as 1 tr), 2 tr into ring, ch 3, * 3 tr into ring, ch 3; rep from * 4 times, join with sl st into 3rd of ch 3. Break off yarn A.

Round 2: Join yarn B to any ch 3 sp, ch 3 (counts as 1 tr), [2 tr, ch 3, 3 tr] into same sp to make corner, * ch 1, [3 tr, ch 3, 3 tr] into next ch 3 sp to make corner; rep from * 4 times, ch 1, join with sl st into 3rd of ch 3. Break off yarn B.

Round 3: Join yarn C to any corner sp, ch 3, [2 tr, ch 3, 3 tr] into same sp, * ch 1, 3 tr into next ch 1 sp, ch 1, [3 tr, ch 3, 3 tr] into next corner sp; rep from * 4 times, ch 1, 3 tr into next ch 1 sp, ch 1, join with sl st into 3rd of ch 3. Break off yarn C.

Round 4: Join yarn B to any corner sp, ch 3, [2 tr, ch 3, 3 tr] into same sp, * [ch 1, 3 tr into each ch 1 sp] along side of hexagon, ch 1, [3 tr, ch 3, 3 tr] into next corner sp; rep from * 4 times, [ch 1, 3 tr into each ch 1 sp] along side of hexagon, ch 1, join with sl st into 3rd of ch 3. Break off yarn B.

Round 5: Join yarn A to any corner sp, ch 3, [2 tr, ch 3, 3 tr] into same sp, * [ch 1, 3 tr into each ch 1 sp] along side of hexagon, ch 1, [3 tr, ch 3, 3 tr] into next corner sp; rep from * 4 times, [ch 1, 3 tr into each ch 1 sp] along side of hexagon, ch 1, join with sl st into 3rd of ch 3.

Round 6: Ch 1, 1 dc into each tr of previous round, working 1 dc into each ch 1 sp along sides of hexagon and 3 dc into each ch 3 corner sp, join with sl st into first dc.

Fasten off yarn.

TUNISIAN CROCHET

Tunisian crochet combines the techniques of both crochet and knitting, and produces a strong, elastic fabric. Tunisian crochet hooks look like long knitting needles with a hook at one end, and they are available in a range of sizes and lengths.

The length of the hook determines how wide the crochet fabric can be. Flexible hooks are also made – these have a short hooked needle joined to a length of flexible cord with a stopper at the end. Flexible hooks come in longer lengths than the ordinary hooks, and enable you to work wider pieces of crochet. Yarn and hook are held in the same way as for ordinary crochet.

WORKING PLAIN TUNISIAN STITCH

Tunisian crochet fabric is made on a foundation chain, and each row is worked in two stages. In the first stage, the loop row, a series of loops are made onto the needle, then on the return row the loops are worked off the needle in pairs without turning the work. Plain Tunisian stitch (below) is the simplest stitch. Other stitches are variations and are made by inserting the hook in different positions, and changing how the loops are worked.

1 Make a crochet foundation chain in the usual way. Insert the hook into the back loop of the second chain, wrap the yarn over the hook and draw a loop through the chain so you have two loops on the hook.

2 Insert the hook into the back loop of the third chain, wrap the yarn over the hook, and draw a loop through so you have three loops on the hook.

3 Repeat along the row until you have made a loop from each chain and have a row of loops on the hook. Do not turn the work.

See also: **Basic Skills, page 12**

4 Wrap the yarn over the hook and draw it through the first loop on the hook. Wrap the yarn over the hook and draw it through the next two loops on the hook. Continue working from left to right, working off two loops at a time until you have only one loop left on the hook.

6 Insert the hook under the next vertical bar, wrap the yarn over the hook and draw a loop through so you have three loops on the hook. Repeat along the row until you have a row of loops on the hook. Do not turn the work.

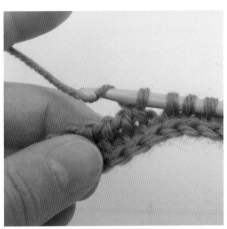

7 To work the return row, wrap the yarn over the hook and draw it through the first loop on the hook, then work off the row of loops in the same way as step 4, leaving one loop on the hook at the end of the row. Repeat from step 5 for length required, ending with a return row.

5 To work the second row, skip the first vertical bar and insert the hook from right to left under the next vertical bar, wrap the yarn over the hook and draw through to make a loop on the hook so you have two loops on the hook.

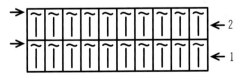

The width of your Tunisian crochet is determined by the length of the hook.

This symbol chart shows how to work plain Tunisian stitch (see page 90 for Stitch Key).

FINISHING THE TOP EDGE OF TUNISIAN CROCHET

After working a piece of Tunisian crochet, finish off the top edge with a row of double crochet to neaten and strengthen the edge.

1 Wrap the yarn over the hook and draw it through the first loop on the hook to make a chain.

2 Insert the hook from right to left under the second vertical bar, wrap the yarn round the hook and draw a loop through so you have two loops on the hook.

3 Wrap the yarn over the hook again and draw it through both loops on the hook to complete the double crochet.

4 Work a double crochet under each vertical bar of the row, then fasten off the yarn.

STITCH COLLECTION

STITCH KEY

Plain Tunisian stitch	
Tunisian knit stitch	
Tunisian mesh stitch	
Loop row	←
Return Row	→

TUNISIAN KNIT STITCH

This variation looks like knitted stockinette stitch on the right side, but the fabric is thicker and more substantial than stockinette stitch. You may find that you need to use a larger hook when working this stitch.

Foundation chain: Work the required number of chains plus 1.

Row 1: (loop row) Insert hook in second ch from hook, YO, draw lp through, *[insert hook in next ch, YO, draw lp through]; rep from * to end, leaving all lps on hook. Do not turn.

Row 1: (return row) YO, draw through one lp on hook, * [YO, draw through 2 lps on hook]; rep from * to end, leaving last lp on hook.

Row 2: (loop row) Sk first vertical bar, insert hook from front to back through next vertical bar, YO, draw lp through, * [insert hook from front to back through next vertical bar, YO, draw lp through]; rep from * to end, leaving all lps on hook. Do not turn.

Row 2: (return row) YO, draw through one lp on hook, * [YO, draw through 2 lps on hook]; rep from * to end, leaving last lp on hook.

Rep row 2 for length required, ending with return row.

To finish the top edge, work as shown on page 90, but insert the hook from front to back through each vertical bar.

Fasten off yarn.

TUNISIAN MESH STITCH

This variation makes a lovely, lacy fabric with good drape, perfect for making a baby blanket or shawl.

Foundation chain: Work the required number of chains plus 1.

Row 1: (loop row) Insert hook in third ch from hook, YO, draw lp through, ch 1, * [insert hook in next ch, YO, draw lp through, ch 1]; rep from * to end, leaving all lps on hook. Do not turn.

Row 1: (return row) YO, draw through one lp on hook, * [YO, draw through 2 lps on hook]; rep from * to end, leaving last lp on hook.

Row 2: (loop row) Ch 1, sk first vertical bar, * [insert hook under horizontal bar slightly above and behind next vertical bar, YO, draw lp through, ch 1]; rep from * to end, leaving all lps on hook. Do not turn.

Row 2: (return row) YO, draw through one lp on hook, * [YO, draw through 2 lps on hook]; rep from * to end, leaving last lp on hook.

Rep row 2 for length required, ending with return row.

To finish the top edge, work as shown on page 90, but insert the hook under the horizontal bar slightly above and behind the next vertical bar.

Fasten off yarn.

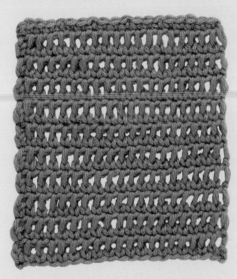

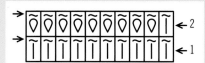

BROOMSTICK CROCHET

Broomstick crochet is worked with an ordinary crochet hook and a large knitting needle, and makes a soft, very lacy fabric.

The length of the knitting needle determines the width of the crochet fabric, so you may need to make several strips and sew them together to get the desired width. This technique is used to make shawls, scarves, wraps and blankets, and it looks good worked in a smooth woollen yarn or a soft mohair.

WHICH SIDE TO USE
Use either the smooth side (above, top) or the ridged side (above, bottom) as the right side of your broomstick crochet fabric.

WORKING BROOMSTICK CROCHET
Each row of broomstick crochet is worked in two stages. In the first stage, the loop row, a series of loops are worked and transferred on to the needle. On the return row, all the loops are slipped off the needle, then crocheted together to make groups. For the beginner, it's best to make a two-row foundation as shown below, but the more experienced crocheter can work the first row directly into a foundation chain.

1 Make a foundation chain to the width required, making sure you have a multiple of five stitches plus turning chain, then turn and work a row of double crochet into the chain.

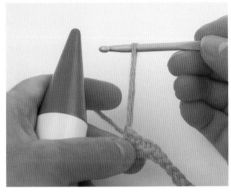

2 Begin the loop row – hold the knitting needle securely under your left arm, extend the loop already on the crochet hook and slip it over the needle.

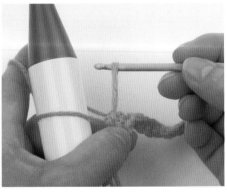

3 Insert the hook into the second stitch, wrap the yarn and draw a loop through, then extend the loop and slip it onto the needle.

See also: **Basic Skills, page 12**

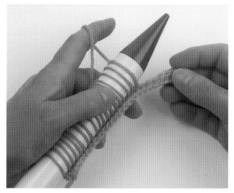

4 Draw a loop through each stitch of the foundation row in the same way to finish the loop row. Check that the number of loops is a multiple of five.

6 Wrap the yarn and draw a loop through the centre of the five-loop group and make one chain.

8 To work the next loop row, do not turn the work. Extend the first loop over the needle as before and repeat the loop row as above. Continue working alternate loop and return rows until the fabric is the required length, ending with a return row.

5 Begin the return row – slip all the loops off the needle and hold the work in your left hand. Insert the hook from right to left through the first five loops.

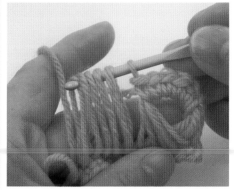

7 Work five double crochet stitches through the centre of the loops. Continue along the row of loops in the same way, grouping five loops together and working five double crochet stitches through the centre of the loops to complete the first return row.

TIP

You may find that broomstick crochet is rather fiddly to work at first, especially when working the loop rows. Gripping the knitting needle between your knees instead of holding it under your arm can help.

HAIRPIN CROCHET

Hairpin crochet (also called hairpin lace and hairpin braid) is worked with an ordinary crochet hook and a special hairpin tool. The technique makes strips of very lacy crochet, which are often used to decorate the edges of ordinary crochet.

Hairpin tools are adjustable, so you can make different widths of crochet. The metal pins are held in position by plastic clips or bars at the top and bottom, and they can be placed close together to make a narrow strip or moved further apart to make wide strips.

A series of loops are made between the two pins using the yarn and the crochet hook until the tool is full of loops. At this point, the loops are taken off the pins, leaving the final few loops attached so that work can continue. When the strip reaches the desired length, all the loops are taken off the tool. You can use the hairpin crochet exactly as it comes off the tool, or you can work a row of double crochet along each looped edge if you prefer.

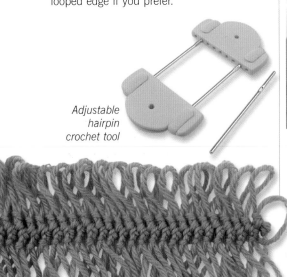

Adjustable hairpin crochet tool

Hairpin crochet

WORKING HAIRPIN LACE

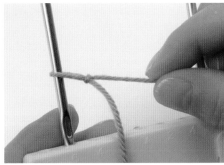

1 Arrange the pins in the bottom clip so they are the required distance apart. Make a slip knot in the yarn and loop it over the left-hand pin.

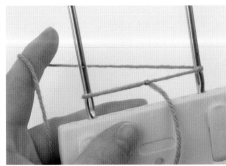

2 Ease the knot across so it lies in the centre between the pins. Take the yarn back around the right-hand pin, tensioning it between your fingers as if you were working ordinary crochet.

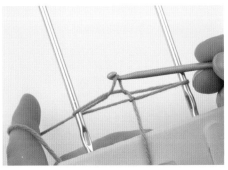

3 Insert the crochet hook into the loop on the left-hand pin, wrap the yarn over the hook and draw it through the loop.

4 Wrap the yarn over the hook again and draw it through the loop on the hook to secure the yarn.

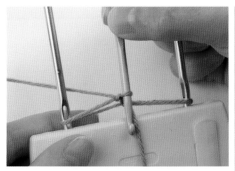

5 Holding the hook vertically, turn the hairpin tool 180° clockwise to make a half turn. The yarn is now wound round the right-hand pin and the other side of the clip is facing you.

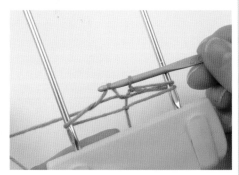

6 Insert the hook under the front loop on the left-hand pin, pick up the yarn at the back of the tool and draw a loop of yarn through so there are two loops on the hook.

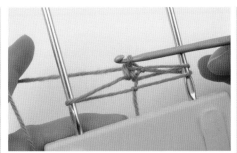

7 Wrap the yarn over the hook and draw through the two loops on the hook to make a double crochet stitch.

8 Repeat steps 5, 6 and 7 until the hairpin tool is filled with braid, remembering to turn the tool clockwise each time.

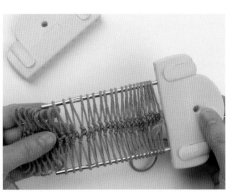

9 When the tool is full, put the top clip onto the pins, remove the lower clip and slide the crochet strip downwards, leaving the last few loops on the pins.

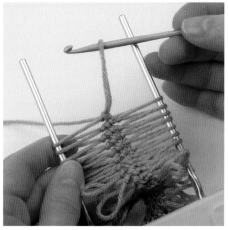

10 Reinsert the lower clip, remove the top clip and continue working the strip as above. When the strip is the required length, pull the yarn end through the last stitch with the hook and slide the strip off the pins.

11 To work an edging, make a slip knot on the hook, insert the hook into the first loop along one edge and work a double crochet stitch. Keeping the loops twisted in the same way they came off the pins, work a double crochet into each loop along the edge, then fasten off the yarn. Repeat along the second edge.

TIP

If you find it difficult to keep the work centred between the pins, it can help if you secure the yarn end to the clip with a piece of masking tape after you've centred the knot in step 2.

MAKING CORDS

Crochet cords can be made in several different ways. They can be flat or rounded, narrow or generously wide. They make handles and shoulder straps for purses, and ties to secure a neckline or the front of a garment. Several lengths of narrow cord can be sewn onto a plain piece of crochet to decorate it with shapes such as spirals, stripes or swirls.

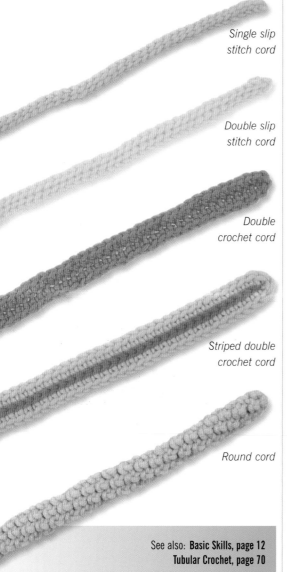

Single slip stitch cord

Double slip stitch cord

Double crochet cord

Striped double crochet cord

Round cord

See also: **Basic Skills, page 12**
Tubular Crochet, page 70

When making a crochet cord, you'll need to make the foundation chain longer than the finished cord you require, because the chain will contract as you work into it. Make several more centimetres of chain than you think you'll need.

These are the quickest and easiest ways of making narrow yet substantial cords, which are good for making ties and using as decoration. The double slip stitch cord is wider than the single slip stitch version.

MAKING A SINGLE SLIP STITCH CORD

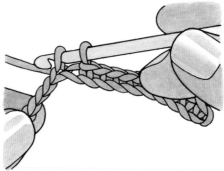

Work a foundation chain to the required length. Change to a size smaller hook, insert into the second chain from the hook and work a row of slip stitch along the top of the chain. You can alter the effect by working the slip stitch row into the back loops of the chain rather than into the top loops.

MAKING A DOUBLE SLIP STITCH CORD

Work a foundation chain to the required length. Change to a size smaller hook, insert into the second chain from the hook and work a row of slip stitch along each side of the chain, turning with one chain at the end of the first side.

TIP

You may need to go down several hook sizes when making slip stitch cords. Aim to make your cord fairly stiff, not loose and floppy.

MAKING A DOUBLE CROCHET CORD

This makes a flat cord which is wider than either of the previous two. You can leave the cord plain or add a contrasting row of crochet down the centre for added interest.

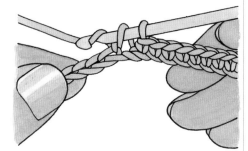

1 Work a foundation chain to the required length. Change to a size smaller hook, insert into the second chain from the hook and work a row of double crochet stitches along one side of the chain.

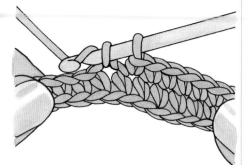

2 At the end of the first side, work one chain, turn, and continue along the second side of the chain in the same way.

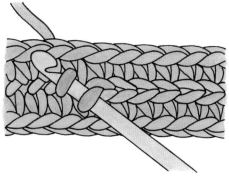

3 Using a contrasting yarn, work a row of slip stitch down the centre of the cord. You may need to use a larger hook size for the contrasting yarn to prevent the stitches from puckering.

MAKING A ROUND CORD

Unlike the other types of crochet cord, this one is worked round and round in a continuous spiral of double crochet until the cord is the required length. It makes a chunky cord, which is good for purse handles and straps.

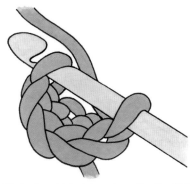

1 Chain 5 and join into a ring with slip stitch. Chain 1 and work a double crochet into the top loop of the next chain.

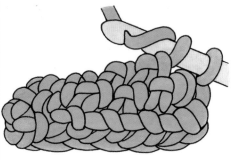

2 Work 1 double crochet into the top loop of each chain, then continue working round and round, making 1 double crochet into the top loop of each stitch. As you work, the cord will begin to appear and will twist slightly in a spiral.

3 When the cord reaches the required length, fasten off the yarn. Thread the yarn end into a yarn needle, catch the top loop of each stitch with the needle and draw up the stitches to close the end of the spiral. Darn in the yarn end to finish. Close the end at the beginning of the spiral in the same way.

MAKING SEW-ON TRIMS

Spiral and flower trims are quick to make, look great and can add the finishing, personal touch to all sorts of household items or garments.

Use a crochet spiral to trim a key-ring or the tab on a zip. You can make a large cluster of trims to decorate each corner of a crochet throw as a novel alternative to a tassel. Decorate garments and accessories with single flowers or work several using different colours and yarns and arrange them in a group.

MAKING A PLAIN SPIRAL

1 Work a loose foundation chain of 30 stitches. Change to a size smaller hook and work two treble crochet stitches into the 4th chain from the hook. Continue along the chain working four treble crochet stitches into each chain.

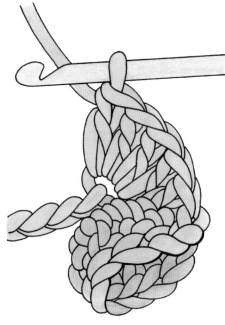

2 As you work, the crochet will begin to twist into a spiral formation naturally. Fasten off the yarn at the end of the row, leaving a yarn end of about 30 cm (12 in) to attach the spiral.

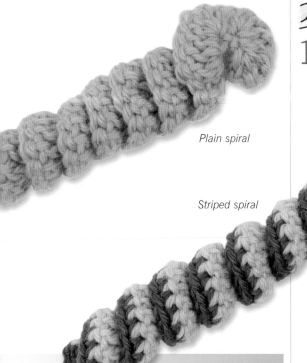

Plain spiral

Striped spiral

See also: **Basic Skills, page 12**

TIF

Experiment with different-shaped yarn combinations. Try working a striped spiral in smooth yarn and edging it with a row of fluffy mohair or angora yarn.

MAKING A STRIPED SPIRAL

MAKING A FRILLED FLOWER

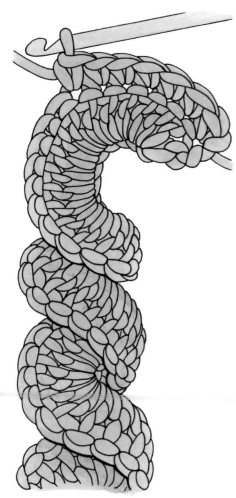

1 Make the base of the first petal by working the required stitches into the ring, then turn the work over so the wrong side is facing you.

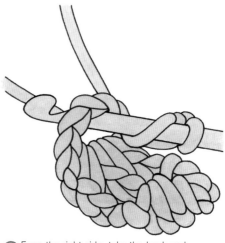

3 From the right side, take the hook and working yarn behind the petal just worked, and then work the first stitch of the new petal into the ring. This will fold the petal into a three-dimensional shape. Continue working the rest of the round as instructed in the pattern.

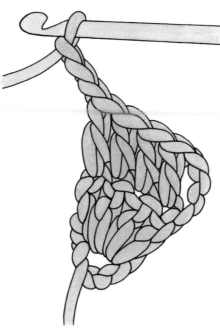

Using one colour of yarn, work a plain spiral as above, leaving a long end for attaching the finished spiral. Join a contrasting yarn to the outer edge of the top of the spiral and work a row of double crochet stitches along the edge. Fasten off the ends of the contrasting yarn.

2 Work the remaining section of petal into the base, chain three and turn the work so the right side is facing you once more.

Frilled flower

MAKING A LAYERED FLOWER

1 Work the first round into the ring, making eight central spokes to form the centre of the flower.

2 Work the first round of petals into the chain spaces between the spokes. At the end of this round, break off the yarn and darn the end of the first colour neatly on the wrong side.

3 Make a slip knot on the hook with the second colour and, working on the wrong side of the flower, insert the hook under one of the central spokes and slip stitch to join. Continue working the next round in the second colour as instructed in the pattern.

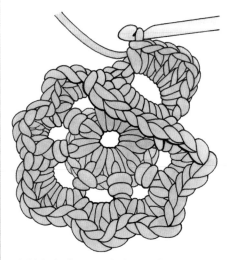

4 Work the final round of petals from the right side of the flower, folding over the petals you made on round 2 to keep them out of the way of the hook.

Layered flower

TIP

Combine textured and metallic yarns to make really unusual flowers.

STITCH COLLECTION

STITCH KEY

Foundation row	F R
Chain	o
Slip stitch	•
Double crochet	+
Half treble crochet	T
Treble crochet	⌐
Treble crochet around spoke	J
Direction of working	⤸
Fasten off	◀
Join new colour	◁
3 chains at end of petal join to first stitch of next petal	⌐⌐o

FRILLED FLOWER

Pretty frilled petals make up this one-round flower. Each petal is completed and then folded over to make the frilled effect. Vary the effect by working the flower in a handpainted yarn rather than a solid colour.

Foundation ring: Ch 6 and join with sl st into a ring.

Round 1: Ch 3 (counts as 1 tr), 3 tr into ring, ch 3, turn; 1 tr into first tr, 1 tr into each of next 2 tr, 1 tr into 3rd of ch 3 (petal made), ch 3, turn; * working across back of petal just made, work 4 tr into ring, ch 3, turn; 1 tr into first tr, 1 tr into each of next 3 tr (petal made), ch 3, turn; rep from * 6 times, join round with sl st into 3rd of beg ch 3 of first petal.

Fasten off yarn.

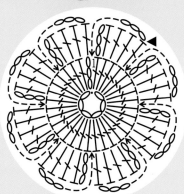

LAYERED FLOWER

Worked in two colours, A and B, this flower looks pretty when two different yarn types are used – experiment with combining a metallic yarn with a mohair yarn. The lower round of petals is worked behind the previous one to give a three-dimensional effect.

Foundation ring: Using yarn A, ch 6 and join with sl st into a ring.

Round 1: Ch 5 (counts as 1 tr, ch 2), [1 tr into ring, ch 2] 7 times, join with sl st into 3rd of ch 5.

Round 2: Sl st into next ch 2 sp, ch 1, [1 dc, 1 htr, 1 tr, 1 htr, 1 dc] into same sp (petal made), [1 dc, 1 htr, 1 tr, 1 htr, 1 dc] into each rem ch sp, join with sl st into first dc.

Break off yarn A.

On the WS, join yarn B to one of the central spokes.

Round 3: Using yarn B and working on the WS, ch 6 (counts as 1 tr, ch 3), [1 tr round next spoke, ch 3] 7 times, join with sl st into 3rd of ch 6.

Round 4: Ch 1, turn flower to RS, working behind petals of round 2, [1 dc, ch 1, 3 tr, ch 1, 1 dc] into next ch 3 sp (petal made), [1 dc, ch 1, 3 tr, ch 1, 1 dc] into each rem ch 3 sp, join with sl st to first dc.

Fasten off yarn.

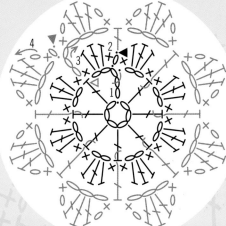

WORKING EDGE FINISHES

Edge finishes differ from crochet edgings and borders in the way that they are worked. An edge finish is worked directly into the crochet fabric, unlike an edging, which is worked separately and then attached.

The basic edge finish is a row of double crochet stitches, and this is often worked as a base before other, more decorative, edgings are worked. Crab stitch edging (also known as reversed double crochet) makes a hardwearing knotted edge, shell edging adds a pretty, feminine finish to garments, and picot edging makes a delicately toothed edge.

WORKING DOUBLE CROCHET EDGING

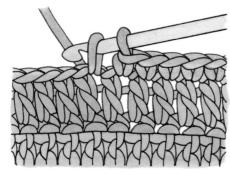

Working from right to left along the row, make a row of ordinary double crochet stitches into the edge of the crochet fabric, spacing the stitches evenly along the edge.

WORKING CRAB STITCH EDGING

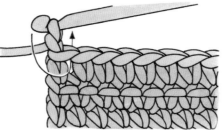

1 Unlike most other crochet techniques, this stitch is worked from left to right along the row. Keeping the yarn at the back of the work, insert the hook from front to back into the next stitch.

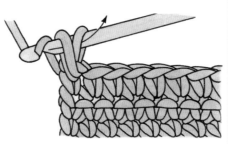

2 Wrap the yarn over the hook and draw the loop through from back to front so there are now two loops on the hook. Wrap the yarn over the hook, then draw the yarn through both loops to complete the stitch.

WORKING SHELL EDGING

1 Work a foundation row of double crochet, a multiple of 6 stitches plus 1, chain 1 and turn. Working from right to left along the row, work 1 double crochet into the first stitch, * skip 2 stitches and work 5 treble crochet stitches into the next stitch to make a shell.

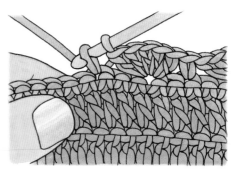

2 Skip 2 stitches, work a double crochet into the next stitch. Repeat from * along the edge.

See also: **Basic Skills, Page 12**
Braids, Edgings and Fringes, Page 106

WORKING PICOT EDGING

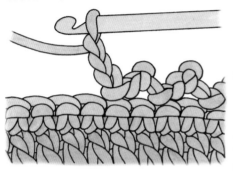

1 With wrong side facing, work a row of an even number of double crochet along the edge and turn. * To start making a picot, chain 3.

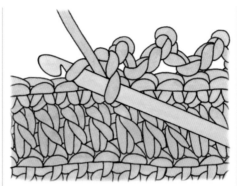

2 Insert the hook into the back of the third chain from the hook and work a slip stitch into it.

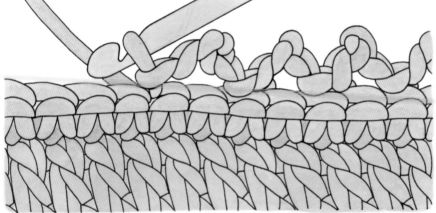

3 Working from right to left along the row, skip one stitch along the double crochet edge and work a slip stitch into the next double crochet. Repeat from * along the edge.

Double crochet edging

Crab stitch edging

Shell edging

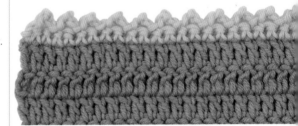

Picot edging

WORKING BUTTONHOLES AND BUTTON LOOPS

Bands with buttons, buttonholes and loops are best worked in double crochet for strength and neatness.
Button loops are a decorative alternative to the ordinary buttonhole, especially for lacy garments.

Make the button band first, mark the positions of the buttons with safety pins and work the buttonhole (or button loop) band to match, making holes or loops opposite the safety-pin markers.

WORKING BUTTONHOLES

To begin making a buttonhole band, work a row of evenly-spaced double crochet along the garment edge, with the right side of the garment facing you. Work further rows of double crochet until the band is the required width for positioning the buttonholes, about half of the total width of the button band, ending with a wrong side row.

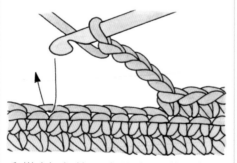

1 Work in double crochet to the position of the buttonhole, skip a few stitches to accommodate the size of the button and work the same number of chains over the skipped stitches.

2 Anchor the chain by working a double crochet stitch after the skipped stitches. Continue in this way along the band until all the buttonholes have been worked.

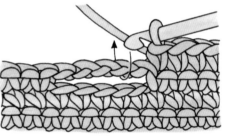

3 On the return (wrong side) row, work a double crochet into each stitch and work the same number of stitches into each chain loop as there are chains.

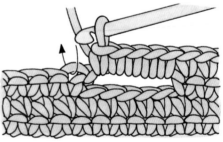

4 Work further rows of double crochet until the buttonhole band is the same width as the button band.

See also: **Basic Skills, page 12**

WORKING BUTTON LOOPS

To begin making a band for button loops, work a row of evenly-spaced double crochet along the garment edge, with the right side of the garment facing you. Work further rows of double crochet until the band is the required width, ending with a wrong side row. Bands for button loops are usually narrower than those with buttonholes.

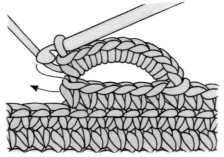

3 To complete the loop, work a series of double crochet stitches into the loop until the chain is completely covered.

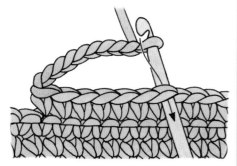

Work in double crochet to the position of the loop then work several more stitches. Work a loop of chains to accommodate the button and turn it towards the right. Slip the hook out of the chain and insert it back into the crochet at the point where you want the loop to finish.

4 Insert the hook into the last double crochet worked before making the chain and work a slip stitch. Continue along the row in double crochet until all the loops have been worked.

2 Insert the tip of the hook into the last chain, wrap the yarn over the hook and join the loop to the band with a slip stitch.

TIP

Don't forget to space out all the buttons at equal intervals on the buttonband first, then mark the positions of the corresponding buttonholes or loops on the opposite band to match.

BRAIDS, EDGINGS AND FRINGES

Braids, edgings and fringes are strips of crochet that can be stitched to other pieces of crochet or to woven fabrics to decorate the edges.

BRAIDS

Braids are narrow, both edges are usually shaped rather than straight and some braid patterns, such as two-colour braid, below, may be worked in more than one colour of yarn. When made from fine cotton, cotton blend or metallic yarns, using a small hook, the effect is similar to the purchased braids used to decorate home furnishings such as lampshades, pillows and fabric-covered boxes and baskets. Hand stitch a braid to fabric using tiny stitches down the centre, or along each edge with a matching sewing thread. Provided the glue is compatible with the fibre composition of the yarn, you can use a glue gun to attach the braid to a box or basket.

2 Fancy braid patterns worked in two or more colours usually have a foundation made in one colour and the trim in a contrasting colour. Work the first row of the contrasting trim along the top of the foundation, along the opposite side to the foundation chain.

WORKING BRAIDS

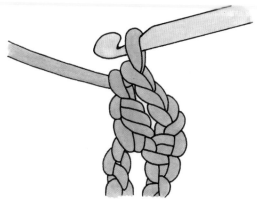

1 Many braids are worked widthways on a small number of stitches. Keep turning the braid and repeating the pattern row until it is the required length, then fasten off the yarn.

3 Break off the contrasting yarn and rejoin it on the other side of the foundation, then work this side to match the one already worked.

STITCH COLLECTION

STITCH KEY

Foundation row F R

Chain ⟳

Slip stitch ·

Double crochet +

Treble crochet ⊤

Fasten off ◀

Join in new colour ◁

INTERWOVEN BRAID (WORKED WIDTHWAYS)

Foundation ring: Ch 7 and join with sl st to form a ring.

Foundation row: Ch 3, 3 tr into ring, ch 3, 1 dc into ring, turn.

Row 1: Ch 3, 3 tr into ch 3 sp, ch 3, 1 dc into same ch 3 sp, turn.

Rep row 1 for length required.

TWO-COLOUR BRAID (WORKED LENGTHWAYS)

Notes: This braid is worked in two colours, yarn A and yarn B.

Foundation chain: Using yarn A, work a multiple of 3 chains.

Foundation row: 1 tr into 6th ch from hook, 1 tr into next ch, * ch 1, sk next ch, 1 tr into each of next 2 chs; rep from * ending last rep with ch 1, sk next ch, 1 tr into last ch.

Break off yarn A.

Join yarn B into penultimate ch of beg skipped ch.

Row 2: Ch 1, 1 dc into first ch sp, ch 3, 2 tr into same ch sp, * [1 dc, ch 3, 1 dc] into next ch 1 sp; rep from * ending last rep with 1 dc into last tr.

Break off yarn B.

Rejoin yarn B to opposite side of braid with sl st into foundation ch below first tr.

Row 3: Ch 1, 1 dc into first ch sp, ch 3, 2 tr into same ch sp, * [1 dc, ch 3, 1 dc] into next ch 1 sp; rep from * ending last rep with 1 dc into 2nd ch of last ch sp.

Fasten off yarn.

EDGINGS

Edgings usually have one straight and one shaped edge. Deep edgings are also known as borders. Edgings can be worked in short rows across the width or in long rows across the length. When working edgings in long rows, it's a good idea to make a longer chain than you think you will need and unravel the unused chains after the edging is finished.

USING AN APPROXIMATE FOUNDATION CHAIN

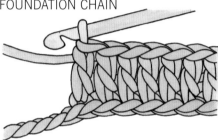

1 Make the foundation chain and work the appropriate number of repeats of your edging pattern. At this point, turn and continue the pattern, leaving any surplus chains unworked.

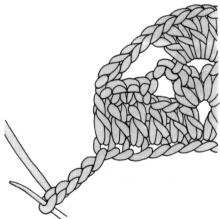

2 When the border is complete, snip off the slip knot at the end of the unworked chains. Using a yarn needle, carefully unravel the chains until you reach the edge of the work, then darn the yarn end in on the wrong side.

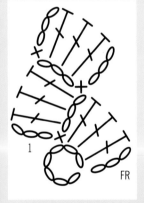

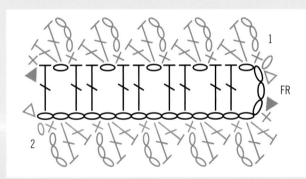

Interwoven braid

Two-colour braid

STITCH COLLECTION

SHELL EDGING (WORKED LENGTHWAYS)

Foundation chain: Work a multiple of 10 chains plus 3.

Foundation row: (RS) 1 tr into 4th ch from hook, 1 tr into each ch to end.

Row 1: Ch 1, 1 dc into each of first 3 tr, * ch 2, sk next 2 tr, [2 tr, ch 2] twice into next tr, sk next 2 tr, 1 dc into each of next 5 tr; rep from * to end omitting 2 dc at end of last rep and working last dc into top of beg skipped ch 3, turn.

Row 2: Ch 3, 1 dc into each of first 2 dc, * ch 3, sk next ch 2 sp, [3 tr, ch 2, 3 tr] into next ch 2 sp, ch 3, sk next dc, 1 dc into each of next 3 dc; rep from * to end omitting 1 dc at end of last rep.

Fasten off yarn.

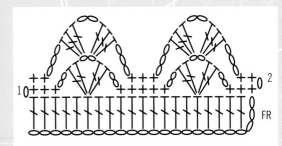

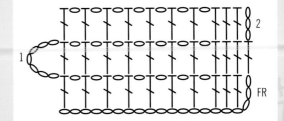

DEEP MESH EDGING (WORKED WIDTHWAYS)

Foundation chain: Ch 20.

Foundation row: (RS) 1 tr into 4th ch from hook, 1 tr into each of next 2 chs, * ch 1, sk next ch, 1 tr into next ch; rep from * to end, turn.

Row 1: Ch 7, 1 tr into first tr, [ch 1, 1 tr into next tr] 7 times, 1 tr into each of next 2 tr, 1 tr into top of beg skipped ch 3, turn.

Row 2: Ch 3 (counts as 1 tr), 1 tr into each of next 3 tr, * ch 1, 1 tr into next tr; rep from * to end, turn.

Row 3: Ch 7, 1 tr into first tr, [ch 1, 1 tr into next tr] 7 times, 1 tr into each of next 2 tr, 1 tr into top of 3rd of ch 3, turn.

Rep rows 2 & 3 for desired length, ending with a row 3.

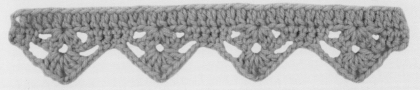

STITCH KEY

Foundation row   F R

Chain   ⌒

Double crochet   +

Treble crochet   ⌡

FRINGES

As a change from the usual yarn fringe of the type found on scarves, try making one of these crochet fringes. The fringe on Chain fringe is made from loops of crochet chain; on the Corkscrew fringe, it's made from strips of double crochet worked so they curl round and round.

WORKING A CROCHET CHAIN FRINGE

On the fringe row, chain 15 and join the end of the chain with a slip stitch into the same place as the previous double crochet stitch.

WORKING A CORKSCREW FRINGE

To make the corkscrew shapes, chain 15 and turn. Work two double crochet stitches into the 2nd chain from the hook and into each remaining chain.

STITCH COLLECTION

CHAIN FRINGE (WORKED LENGTHWAYS)

Foundation chain: Make the required length of foundation chain.

Row 1: 1 dc into 2nd ch from hook, 1 dc into each ch to end, turn.

Row 2: Ch 1, 1 dc into each dc to end, turn.

Row 3: Ch 1, 1 dc into first dc, * 1 dc into next dc, ch 15, sl st into same place as dc just worked; rep from * to end.

Fasten off yarn.

CORKSCREW FRINGE (WORKED LENGTHWAYS)

Foundation chain: Make the required length of foundation chain.

Row 1: 1 dc into 2nd ch from hook, 1 dc into each ch to end, turn.

Row 2: Ch 1, 1 dc into each dc to end, turn.

Row 3: Ch 1, 1 dc into first dc, * 1 dc into next dc, ch 15, turn; working back along the chain, sk first ch, 2 dc into each rem ch, sl st into same place as dc before the ch 15; rep from * to end.

Fasten off yarn.

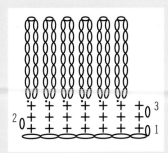

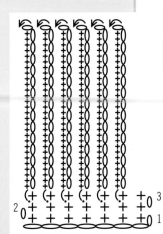

STITCH KEY

Chain	⚬
Double crochet	+
Slip stitch	•
Slip stitch into dc below	(
Turn and work back along chain	↙

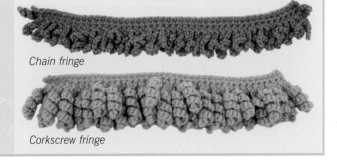

Chain fringe

Corkscrew fringe

SURFACE CROCHET

Surface crochet is exactly as the name suggests, crochet worked on top of a crochet background. You can work on plain double crochet fabric, but the lines of surface slip stitch look much more effective worked on a mesh background.

Choose a smooth yarn to make the mesh background, then you can add rows of contrasting colours and textures to the surface using this simple, but effective technique.

Surface crochet can be worked in contrasting yarn textures.

Try mixing metallic and smooth yarns.

See also: **Openwork and Lace Stitches, page 50**

WORKING SURFACE CROCHET

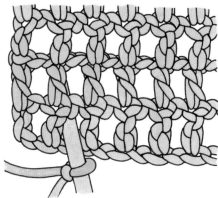

1 Work a mesh background. Make a slip knot in the contrasting yarn and slip it onto the hook. Insert the hook in the mesh through a hole along the lower edge of the mesh.

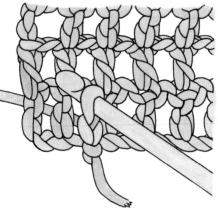

2 Holding the contrasting yarn behind the mesh, draw a loop of yarn through the mesh and through the loop on the hook to make a slip stitch. Continue in this way, working up the mesh and making one slip stitch in each hole.

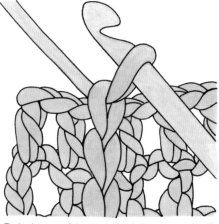

3 At the top of the row, break the yarn and pull it through the last stitch to secure.

TIP

As well as the two mesh background stitches shown here, you can use other crochet stitches as a background for this technique, including double and half treble crochet, but remember not to work the background stitches too tightly.

STITCH COLLECTION

OPENWORK MESH

To make the mesh background, turn to page 50, and work a piece of fabric in the Openwork mesh pattern. Work vertical rows of surface crochet to make solid stripes across the background. This mesh has fairly large holes, so it's a good idea to use a heavier weight of yarn to work the surface crochet than the one you used for the background.

SMALL MESH

This background fabric has much smaller holes than the large mesh shown left. You can work surface crochet in rows on this fabric, but the smaller mesh means you can experiment and work all sorts of random patterns like the one shown here.

Foundation chain: Work a multiple of 2 chains.

Foundation row: (RS) 1 dc into 2nd ch from hook, * ch 1, sk next ch, 1 dc into next ch; rep from * to end, turn.

Row 1: Ch 1, 1 dc into first dc, * ch 1, 1 dc into next dc; rep from * to end, turn.

Rep row 1 for length required.

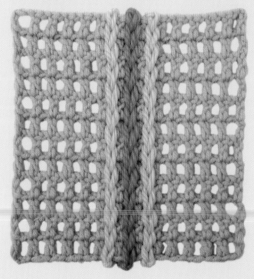

STITCH KEY

Foundation row F R

Chain o

Double crochet +

Treble crochet T

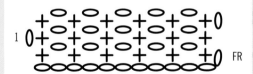

APPLYING BEADS

Beads can be applied to crochet at the same time as the stitches are being worked. They look most effective against a double crochet background, and add touches of colour, as well as sparkle.

Before starting to crochet, thread all the beads onto your ball of yarn. If you're using several balls to make a garment, for example, the pattern instructions will tell you how many beads to thread onto each ball of yarn. When choosing beads, match the size of the holes in the beads to the thickness of your yarn; small beads are best on fine yarns, and larger beads on chunky yarns. When working with different bead colours arranged in a particular pattern, don't forget that you should thread the different colours onto the yarn in reverse order, so the pattern will work out correctly as you crochet. Beads are applied on wrong side rows.

Choose beads to match your yarn.

See also: **Applying Sequins, page 114**

BEADING WITH DOUBLE CROCHET

1 Work to the position of the first bead on a wrong side row. Slide the bead down the yarn until it rests snugly against the right side of your work.

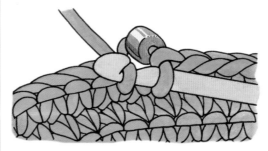

2 Keeping the bead in position, insert hook in next stitch and draw yarn through so there are two loops on the hook.

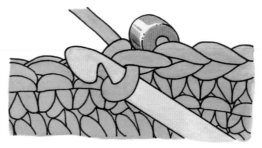

3 Wrap the yarn over the hook again and draw it through to complete the stitch. Continue adding beads in the same way across the row, following the pattern instructions.

STITCH COLLECTION

STITCH KEY

Foundation row F R

Chain ⌀

Double crochet +

Beaded double crochet ◆

ALTERNATE BEADS

Beads of one colour are arranged alternately to make this elegant beaded pattern. Use matte beads, like the ones shown, or choose from metallic and glitter types to add more sparkle.

Note: B = work beaded double crochet stitch. This stitch uses one colour of beads. Thread all the beads onto the yarn before starting to crochet.

Foundation chain: Work a multiple of 6 chains plus 3.

Foundation row: (RS) 1 dc into 2nd ch from hook, 1 dc into each ch to end, turn.

Rows 1 & 2: Ch 1, 1 dc into each dc to end, turn.

Row 3: (WS bead row) Ch 1, 1 dc into each of next 4 dc, * B, 1 dc into each of next 5 dc; rep from * to last 5 sts, B, 1 dc into each of next 4 dc, turn.

Rows 4, 5 & 6: Rep row 1.

Row 7: (WS bead row) Ch 1, 1 dc into first dc, * B, 1 dc into each of next 5 dc; rep from * to last 2 sts, B, 1 dc into last dc, turn.

Rows 8, 9 & 10: Rep row 1.

Rep rows 3–10 for length required, ending with a row 5.

ALL-OVER BEADS

Beads added to every wrong side row make a heavily beaded fabric that would look good when used to make an evening bag. You could also work several rows of this pattern in a narrow band around the hem of a sweater.

Note: B = work beaded double crochet stitch. This stitch uses several colours of beads that are threaded randomly onto the yarn. Thread all the beads onto the yarn before starting to crochet.

Foundation chain: Work a multiple of 4 chains plus 3.

Foundation row: (RS) 1 dc into 2nd ch from hook, 1 dc into each ch to end, turn.

Row 1: (WS bead row) Ch 1, 1 dc into each of next 2 dc, * B, 1 dc into each of next 3 dc; rep from * to last 4 dc, B, 1 dc into each of next 3 dc, turn.

Row 2: Ch 1, 1 dc into each dc to end, turn.

Rows 3 & 4: Rep rows 1 & 2.

Row 5: (WS bead row) Ch 1, 1 dc into each of next 5 dc, * B, 1 dc into each of next 3 dc; rep from * to last 6 dc, B, 1 dc into each of next 5 dc, turn.

Row 6: Ch 1, 1 dc into each dc to end, turn.

Rows 7 & 8: Rep rows 5 & 6.

Rep rows 1–8 for length required, ending with a RS row.

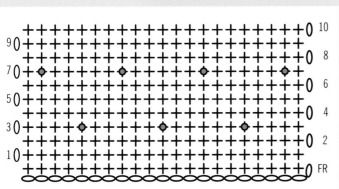

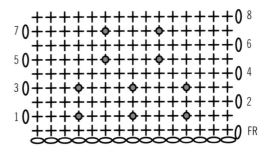

APPLYING SEQUINS

Sequins can be applied to a background of double crochet in a similar way to beads. Round sequins are the best ones to use, either flat or cup-shaped types. As a general rule, thread sequins onto your yarn in the same way as beads.

When crocheting with cup-shaped sequins, make sure you thread them onto the yarn so the convex side of each sequin faces the same way toward the ball of yarn. When crocheted, the "cup" should face away from the crochet fabric; in order to show the sequin from the best advantage and to prevent the sequin damaging the crochet.

Alternate beads pattern (page 113) using sequins instead of beads.

ADDING SEQUINS TO DOUBLE CROCHET

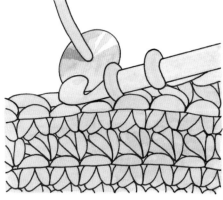

1 Work to the position of the first sequin on a wrong side row. Work the first stage of the double crochet, leaving two loops on the hook. Slide the sequin down the yarn until it rests snugly against the right side of your work. Remember, if you're using cup-shaped sequins, the convex side (the bottom of the cup) should be next to the fabric.

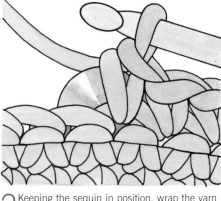

2 Keeping the sequin in position, wrap the yarn round the hook and draw it through to complete the stitch. Continue adding sequins in the same way across the row, following the pattern instructions.

See also: Applying beads, p112

TIP

Knitting sequins have larger holes than ordinary ones and they are often sold threaded onto a loop of strong thread. To use the sequins, cut the loop, knot one end of the thread onto your yarn and carefully slide the sequins over the knot and onto the yarn.

STITCH
COLLECTION

SEQUIN STRIPES

Sequins often look best when used sparingly to accentuate a design. Here, flat, round sequins are arranged in neat vertical rows so that the sequins touch. You can use a contrasting sequin colour or match them to the background for a more subtle effect.

Note: S = work sequinned double crochet stitch. This stitch uses one colour of sequins. Thread all the sequins onto the yarn before starting to crochet.

Foundation chain: Work a multiple of 6 chains plus 3.

Foundation row: (RS) 1 dc into 2nd ch from hook, 1 dc into each ch to end, turn.

Rows 1 & 2: Ch 1, 1 dc into each dc to end, turn.

Row 3: (WS sequin row) Ch 1, 1 dc into each of next 3 dc, * S, 1 dc into each of next 5 dc; rep from * to last 5 sts, S, 1 dc into each of next 4 dc, turn.

Row 4: Ch 1, 1 dc into each dc to end, turn.

Rep rows 3 & 4 for length required, ending with a row 4.

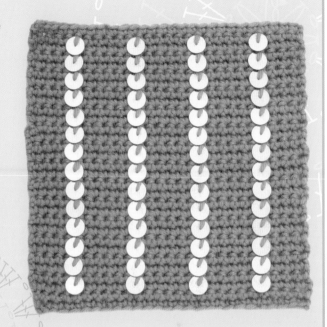

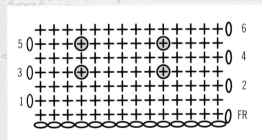

STITCH KEY

Foundation row F R

Chain

Double crochet +

Sequined double crochet

Chapter 3
PROJECTS

This chapter shows you how to make a variety of projects using the skills you have mastered in the two previous chapters. Whether you want to make a small crochet accessory such as a pretty scarf or flower-trimmed bag, or feel ready to try something a little more complicated, there's something here for everyone.

Project 1 / WINTER SCARF

A scarf makes the perfect project for a beginner to crochet. There is no shaping, the work is narrow enough to grow quickly and you can choose to use many of the stitches shown in the Stitch Collections throughout the book. The scarf in the photograph is worked in Fan lace, see page 53, using a pure wool yarn.

YOU WILL NEED
- 2 balls of Jaeger Matchmaker Merino double knitting (or DK weight yarn with 120 m (131 yds) per 50 g ball) in shade 896 rock rose.
- Size F (4 mm) and size G (4.5 mm) crochet hooks or size needed to achieve tension.
- Yarn needle.

TENSION
After blocking, one complete pattern repeat measures 6 cm (2 in) wide and 3 cm (1 in) deep.

FINISHED SIZE
After blocking, scarf measures approximately 18 cm (7 in) wide and 117 cm (46 in) long.

WORKING THE CROCHET
The stitch pattern, Fan lace, requires a multiple of 12 chains plus 3. The scarf in the photograph was worked on a foundation chain of 39 = (12 x 3) + 3.

Using the size G (4.5 mm) hook, make a foundation chain of 39 chains.

Change to the size F (4 mm) hook and work even in pattern for approximately 117 cm (46 in), ending with a row 4.

FINISHING THE SCARF

Darn in all the yarn ends. Block the scarf (see page 26) and allow to dry.

USING A DIFFERENT STITCH

Stitch patterns need a given number of stitches for the pattern to work correctly. When using a different stitch to make the scarf, simply make the foundation chain to the required number and work a strip to the length you require.

OPENWORK MESH (SEE PAGE 51)

This stitch is very easy to work and has good drape. It requires a multiple of 2 chains and the swatch was worked on a foundation chain of 36 chains.

SEASHORE TRELLIS (SEE PAGE 52)

A very pretty pattern which looks good worked in ombré yarn to make a scarf. It requires a multiple of 12 chains plus 3 and the swatch was worked on a foundation chain of 39 chains. This is the same number of chains as the scarf in the photograph, but the swatch is narrower than the scarf, due to the difference in stitch construction.

TRINITY STITCH (SEE PAGE 39)

This cluster pattern makes a denser, heavier swatch than the two previous ones and it would make a warmer scarf than any of the lace stitches. It requires a multiple of 2 chains and the swatch was worked on a foundation chain of 34 chains.

WAVY CHEVRONS (SEE PAGE 60)

Any of the chevron stitches on pages 58 to 61 will make an attractive scarf, whether worked in one colour or striped in several toning or contrasting yarns. Wavy chevrons stitch requires a multiple of 14 chains plus 3 and the swatch was worked on a foundation chain of 45 chains.

TIP

Choose a yarn that feels soft and non-scratchy next to your skin for making a scarf. Pure merino wool and wool/synthetic blends work well.

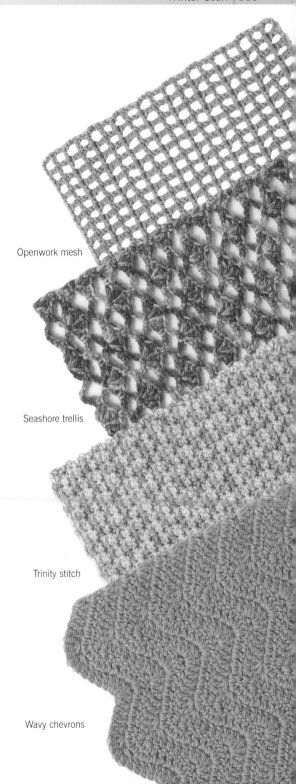

Openwork mesh

Seashore trellis

Trinity stitch

Wavy chevrons

Project 2 / BABY AFGHAN

An afghan for a new baby is always a popular gift. This design is fairly small, but you can easily make it larger simply by adding more motifs before you work the edging. If you do this, remember that you will need to buy more yarn than the amount suggested below.

YOU WILL NEED
- Jaeger Baby Merino double knitting (or DK weight baby yarn with 120 m (131 yds) per 50 g yarn) in 3 coordinating colours:
  1 ball of 223 spring, 2 balls of 202 snowdrop and 205 buttermilk.
- Size E (3.5 mm) and size F (4 mm) crochet hook or size needed to achieve tension.
- Yarn needle.

TENSION
After blocking, each motif measures 14 cm (5 in) square.

FINISHED SIZE
Afghan measures 48 cm (18 in) wide and 72 cm (28 in) long, including edging.

WORKING THE MOTIFS
Following the pattern for the Croydon square motif on page 80 and using size F (4 mm) hook, work eight motifs (motif A on diagram) using snowdrop as yarn A, spring as yarn B and buttermilk as yarn C. Make seven motifs (motif B on diagram) using buttermilk as yarn A, spring as yarn B and snowdrop as yarn C.

The baby afghan is worked in separate square motifs stitched together so it can easily be made larger.

A	B	A	B	A
B	A	B	A	B
A	B	A	B	A

MAKING UP THE AFGHAN

Darn in all the yarn ends. Block each motif (see page 26) and allow to dry. Arrange the motifs as shown in the diagram and stitch together using matching yarn.

WORKING THE EDGING

Using size E (3.5 mm) hook, join buttermilk yarn to any dc along the edge of the afghan.

Round 1: Ch 3, 1 tr into each dc round afghan, working 5 tr into centre stitch of 3 dc group at each corner, join with sl st into 3rd of ch 3.

Break off buttermilk yarn and join snowdrop yarn in same place.

Round 2: Ch 3, 1 tr into each tr of previous round, working 5 tr into centre stitch of 5 tr group at each corner, join with sl st into 3rd of ch 3.

Break off snowdrop yarn and join spring yarn in same place.

Round 3: Ch 1, 1 dc into same place, 1 dc into each tr of previous round, working 3 dc into centre stitch of 5 tr group at each corner, join with sl st into first dc.

Fasten off yarn.

FINISHING

To finish, press edging lightly on wrong side with warm iron or block the afghan again.

Project 3 / FILET CROCHET WRAP

Filet crochet creates a delightful lacy accessory. Worked in rows across the width of the wrap, each end is decorated with a pretty border pattern and the main part of the wrap is in filet mesh, dotted here and there with tiny four-block motifs.

YOU WILL NEED

- 8 balls of Jaeger Matchmaker Merino double knitting (or DK weight yarn with 120 m (131 yds) per 50 g ball) in shade 897 azalea.
- Size F (4 mm) and size G (4.5 mm) crochet hooks or size needed to achieve tension.
- Yarn needle.

TENSION

Measured widthways and lengthways over filet mesh worked using size F (4 mm) hook, approximately eight spaces to 10 cm (4 in).

FINISHED SIZE

Wrap measures approximately 58 cm (23 in) wide and 170 cm (67 in) long.

Filet crochet creates a lacy fabric, perfect for evening wear.

WORKING THE CROCHET

Using size G (4.5 mm) hook, make a foundation chain of 146 chains. Change to size F (4 mm) hook and, following the guidelines for working filet crochet on page 54, work two rows of spaces.

Begin working the border pattern from the chart, repeating the section of the chart inside the red lines six more times. Work upwards from the bottom of the chart, starting at the right-hand edge and reading right side rows (odd-numbered rows) from right to left, and wrong side rows (even-numbered rows) from left to right.

At the end of the border pattern, work in filet mesh, dotting several repeats of the tiny motif from the second chart at random across the mesh. When the work measures approximately 157.5 cm (62 in) long, ending with a WS row, work the border chart once more. Finish by working two rows of spaces to match the opposite end.

FINISHING THE WRAP

Darn in all the yarn ends. Block (see page 26) and allow to dry, or press lightly on the wrong side with a warm iron.

Project 4 / BUTTONHOLE BAG

Brightly-coloured flowers and leaves trim a plain buttonhole bag which is large enough to hold your purse, keys, mobile phone and other essentials. The bag pattern also looks good without the added trimmings, and it can be worked in one colour or in stripes.

YOU WILL NEED
- 4 balls of double knitting weight yarn with approx. 120 m (131 yds) per 50 g ball in a neutral colour.
- Oddments of the same weight of yarn in red, yellow and green.
- Size F (4 mm), size J (6 mm) and size K (6.5 mm) crochet hooks.
- Yarn needle.

FINISHED SIZE
Bag measures 25 cm (10 in) deep and 27 cm (10 in) wide.

TENSION
14 stitches and 17 rows to 10 cm (4 in) measured over double crochet with two strands of main yarn held together using size J (6 mm) crochet hook.

CROCHETING THE BAG FRONT
Holding two strands of main yarn together and using size K (6.5 mm) hook, ch 37. Change to size J (6 mm) hook.
Foundation row: (RS) 1 dc into 2nd ch from hook, 1 dc into each ch to end, turn.
Row 1: Ch 1, 1 dc into each dc of previous row, turn (36 dc).
Rep row 1 31 times, ending with a RS row.

MAKE BUTTONHOLE
Row 1: (WS) Ch 1, 1 dc into each of next 12 dc, ch 12, sk next 12 dc, 1 dc into each of next 12 dc, turn.
Row 2: Ch 1, 1 dc into each of next 12 dc, 1 dc into each of next 12 chs, sk next 12 dc, 1 dc into each of next 12 dc, turn (36 dc).

Decorating with sew-on motifs means you can add as little or as much embellishment to the bag as you like.

MAKING THE HANDLE

Row 1: Ch 1, 1 dc into each dc of previous row, turn.

Rep row 1 three times, ending with a RS row.

Fasten off yarn.

CROCHETING THE BAG BACK

Work as for front.

WORKING THE FLOWERS AND LEAVES

Using contrasting yarn, size F (4 mm) hook and following the instructions for making a Frilled flower (see page 101), make three red and three yellow flowers.

Using green yarn and size F (4 mm) hook, make two short lengths of double crochet cord following the instructions on page 97.

FINISHING THE BAG

Press the pieces lightly on the wrong side (see page 26). Darn in the yarn ends on the wrong side using the yarn needle (see page 23).

Using the photograph as a guide to position, pin flowers and leaves to front of bag, making sure flowers overlap ends of leaves. Secure flowers with a few stitches worked in matching yarn, taking the stitches over the chains behind each flower petal. Stitch leaves in place down the centre of each leaf.

Place the pieces together with right sides facing and pin round the edges. Using the same yarn in the yarn needle, join side and base seams and turn bag to right side.

TIP

Two strands of main yarn are held together throughout; contrasting colours are used singly.

Project 5 / INTARSIA POTHOLDER

Combine odds and ends of double knitting yarn with one ball of main colour and make this cheerful intarsia potholder. The back piece is worked in double crochet using the main colour, but you could work two patterned pieces if you prefer.

YOU WILL NEED

- 1 ball of double knitting yarn with 120 m (131 yds) per 50 g ball in main colour (yarn A).
- Oddments of the same yarn weight in four toning colours, yarns B, C, D and E.
- Size F (4 mm) and size G (4.5 mm) crochet hooks, or size needed to achieve tension.
- Yarn needle.

TENSION

17 stitches and 21 rows to 10 cm (4 in) measured over double crochet, worked with size F (4 mm) crochet hook.

This is the ideal project for using up some of the odds and ends of yarn you have in your stash.

FINISHED SIZE

Potholder measures approximately 19 cm (7 in) square, including edging but excluding hanging loop.

WORKING THE CROCHET

FRONT

Using size G (4.5 mm) hook and yarn A, make a foundation chain of 31 chains. Change to size F (4 mm) hook and following the guidelines for working intarsia on page 68, work the pattern from the chart, reading upwards from the bottom. Start at the right-hand edge and read right side rows (odd-numbered rows) from right to left and wrong side rows (even-numbered rows) from left to right.

When the chart has been completed, fasten off the yarn.

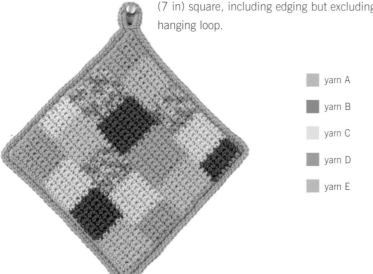

■ yarn A

■ yarn B

■ yarn C

■ yarn D

■ yarn E

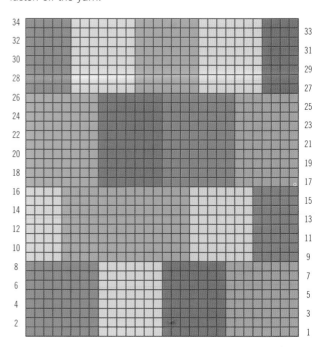

BACK

Using size G (4.5 mm) hook and yarn A,
make a foundation chain of 31 chains.
Change to size F (4 mm) hook.
Foundation row: (RS) 1 dc into second ch
from hook, 1 dc into each ch to end,
turn (30 dc).
Row 1: Ch 1, 1 dc into each
dc on previous row, turn.
Rep row 1 32 times, ending
with a WS row.
Fasten off yarn.

FINISHING THE POTHOLDER

Darn in all the yarn ends (see page 23).
Block each piece (see page 26) to
the same size and allow to dry.
Pin front and back pieces
together with WS facing.
With front piece facing, join yarn A to one
corner of potholder.
Round 1: (RS) Ch 1, 1 dc into same place,
work evenly-spaced round of dc round edge,
working 3 dc into each corner, join with sl st
to first dc.
Round 2: Make hanging loop (ch 9, insert
hook into last st of previous round and work
sl st), ch 1, work 15 dc into loop, work 1 dc
into each dc of previous round, working 3 dc
into centre stitch of 3 dc group at each
corner, join with sl st into first dc of loop.
Fasten off yarn and darn in yarn ends.

Project 6 / HEXAGON PILLOW

Making a pillow cover out of motifs is a great way of showing off your crochet skills. In this pattern, 24 hexagons worked in a neutral palette are joined together to make a rectangular cover. You can use the type of coordinating colour scheme shown here, or work each hexagon in a different colour using up oddments of yarn from your stash.

YOU WILL NEED

- Jamieson's Shetland double knitting (or Shetland DK yarn with 122 m (134 yds) per 50 g ball) in 7 coordinating colours:
  1 x 50 g ball of 425 mustard (A), 478 amber (B), 104 natural white (C) and 350 lemon (G), 2 x 50 g balls of 375 flax (D), 190 tundra (E) and 1200 nutmeg (F).
- Size F (4 mm) crochet hook or size needed to achieve tension.
- Yarn needle.
- Rectangular pillow form 40 x 50 cm (16 x 20 in).

TENSION

After blocking, each motif measures 13 cm (5 in) from side to side and 14.5 cm (5 ¾ in) from point to point.

FINISHED SIZE

Finished cover will fit a 40 x 50 cm (16 x 20 in) pillow form.

WORKING THE MOTIFS

Using the Wheel hexagon pattern on page 86, work three motifs in yarns A, B, C and G; four motifs in yarns D, E and F.

Working hexagonal motifs is a great way to show off your crochet skills.

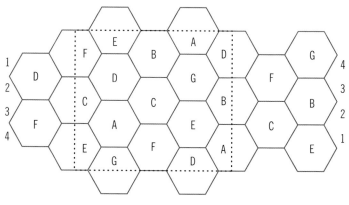

·········· Fold line

MAKING UP THE PILLOW COVER

Darn in all the yarn ends (see page 23).
Block each motif (see page 26) and allow to
dry. Arrange the motifs as shown in the
diagram and stitch together using matching
yarn. When the motifs have been joined, fold
the crochet to the back following the dotted
lines shown on the diagram and join the
opposite edges of the remaining motifs.
Leave the motif edges numbered 1,
2, 3 and 4 on the diagram
unstitched to make the
opening down the back of the
cover. Turn cover to the right
side and insert the pillow
form. Matching the edges of
the motifs down the opening,
pin together and stitch.

Project 7 / STRIPED BAG

Use all sorts of odds and ends of yarn from your stash to make this pretty drawstring bag. To make the bag in the photograph, a selection of double knitting yarns was used including shiny ribbon, metallic chainette, novelty yarn and smooth wool. You can change yarn at the end of every round, or work several rounds in the same yarn – the choice is up to you.

YOU WILL NEED
- A selection of double knitting yarns in varying colours and textures. As a guide, to work one round of treble crochet at the bag's widest point, you'll need about 3.2 m (3 yds) of yarn.
- Size F (4 mm) and size G (4.5 mm) crochet hooks.
- Yarn needle.

Be imaginative with your choice of yarns when creating this bag to make a really unique piece.

TENSION
Working to an exact tension is not necessary when making this project.

FINISHED SIZE
The bag in the photograph measures approximately 33 cm (13 in) from top to bottom and 52 cm (20 in) round the bag at the widest point. The opening round the top of the bag measures 33 cm (13 in).

WORKING THE BAG
Work from the centre of the bag base, using size F (4 mm) hook and following the Treble crochet circle pattern on page 75 for rounds 1–4.

Continue as follows, changing colours as desired.

Round 5: Work as round 4, but work 3 tr between the incs (80 sts).

Round 6: Ch 3, 1 tr into each of next 2 tr, *2 tr into next tr, 1 tr into each of next 4 tr; rep from * to last 2 tr, 2 tr into next tr, 1 tr into last tr, join with sl st into 3rd of ch 3 (96 sts).

Round 7: Ch 1, 1 dc into first tr, 1 dc into each tr of previous round, join with sl st into first dc.

Rounds 8, 9 & 10: Ch 1, 1 dc into first dc, 1 dc into each dc worked on previous round, join with sl st into first dc.

Round 11: Ch 3, sk first dc, 1 tr into each dc of previous round, join with sl st into 3rd of ch 3.

Round 12: Ch 3, sk first tr, 1 tr into each tr of previous round, join with sl st into 3rd of ch 3.

Count in the same way without increasing, working either an dc or tr round as folls.

Rounds 13, 15, 16, 17, 18, 22 & 23: Work round of tr.

Rounds 14, 19, 20 & 21: Work round of dc.

Round 24: Ch 3, 1 tr into each of next 2 tr, *tr2tog, 1 tr into each of next 4 tr; rep from * to last 3 sts, tr2tog, 1 tr into last tr; join with sl st into 3rd of ch 3 (80 sts).

Rounds 25, 26 & 27: Work round of tr.

Round 28: Ch 3, 1 tr into next tr, *tr2tog, 1 tr into each of next 3 tr; rep from * to last 3 sts, tr2tog, 1 tr into last tr, join with sl st into 3rd of ch 3 (64 sts).

Rounds 29, 30, 31 & 32: Work round of tr.

Round 33: Ch 3, 1 tr into each of next 3 tr, *ch 2, sk next 2 tr, 1 tr into each of next 6 tr; rep from * to last 4 sts, ch 2, sk next 2 tr, 1 tr into each of last 2 tr, join with sl st into 3rd of ch 3.

Round 34: Ch 1, 1 dc into first tr, *1 dc into each of next 2 chs, 1 dc into each of next 6 tr; rep from * to last ch 2 sp, 1 dc into each of next 2 chs, 1 dc into each of next 2 tr, join with sl st into first dc.

Rounds 35–40: Work round of dc.

Round 41: Ch 1, work sl st into each st of previous round. Fasten off yarn.

WORKING THE DRAWSTRINGS (MAKE 2)

Using a smooth yarn and size G (4.5 mm) hook, make a foundation chain of 125 chains and work a length of double crochet cord following the instructions on page 97.

FINISHING THE BAG

Darn in all the yarn ends. Press lightly on the wrong side if necessary with a cool iron. Thread the two drawstrings through the holes in the purse, pulling the ends free at opposite sides of the purse. Stitch across the short ends of each drawstring and darn in the yarn ends.

Chapter 4
GALLERY

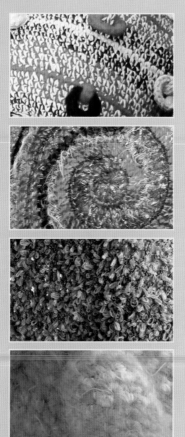

Drawn from a variety of sources across the world, the Gallery features a wide range of crochet garments, accessories and other items designed to inspire and challenge you with new ideas. Dip into a bounty of colour, shape, pattern and texture and investigate some of the possibilities offered by the wonderful craft of crochet.

Crocheted garments

Crochet can be used to create a wide variety of garments, ranging from delicate lacy items for evening wear to a traditional warm but stylish sweater for everyday wear. Crochet stitches can be worked to a set pattern or they can be employed in a more adventurous way to make one-of-a-kind freeform wearables.

◀ SPIRAL SWEATER WRAP
Kristin Omdahl

Based on a large spiral shape centred across the back, the construction of this garment is somewhere between a sweater and a wrap. It is crocheted in natural shades of pure alpaca yarn, and has ribbed sleeves and a picot trim round the edge.

▶ FREEFORM RED SWEATER
Margaret Hubert

Freeform crochet (also called scumbling) combines small pieces of crochet which are joined together as you work. The technique features frequent changes of stitches, textures and colours and every garment is unique.

▲ IVORY COTTON DRESS
Kazekobo (Yoko Hatta)

Worked in fine ivory cotton,
this gorgeous openwork dress
is decorated with elaborate
crochet layered flowers,
bunches of grapes and leaves.
A scalloped edging trims the
hemline and the garment is
lined in ivory silk fabric.

◀ JACKET AND STRIPED SKIRT
Kazekobo (Yoko Hatta)

A fun and funky outfit of an
orange mohair buttoned top with
elbow-length sleeves, teamed with
a slim striped skirt in coordinating
colours of wool. There's lots of
attention to detail here,
particularly the tied cords trimmed
with tassels.

Hats, scarves and mittens

Crochet is ideal for making cosy and practical winter hats, mittens and scarves. But why stop there? A frilled edge, bobbles, tassels or cords can transform your creations into fun and fashionable accessories. Explore the possibilities offered by novelty yarns such as eyelash, chenille, boucle and mohair to add textural interest to your crochet.

◀ USHANKA
Lajla Nuhic

A warm and wonderful hat for winter with cosy earflaps and ties. The top section is worked in a mohair, wool and nylon blend, the lower section in hand-dyed cotton chenille. The spiral decoration was added in double crochet after the hat was finished.

◀ RINGS
Lajla Nuhic

Worked in double crochet with two strands of fine crochet yarn held together throughout, this delightful hat is decorated with separate crocheted rings held in place on the surface by loops of double crochet.

▶ TUNISIAN SCARF
Jennifer Hansen

Worked lengthways in Tunisian crochet, this scarf is made from bulky yarn and features lots of colour changes. The yarn ends were not darned into the scarf, but left dangling to form a simple fringe.

▲ STRIPED MITTENS
Carol Meldrum

Crocheted in chunky weight yarn in two-colour stripes of double crochet, these mittens are worked using a smaller than usual size hook to make a sturdy, compact fabric to keep hands warm.

▶ ZIGZAG SCARF
Jan Eaton

Worked lengthways in a simple ripple stitch, this highly-textured scarf combines thin, thick, textured and novelty yarns based around a colour palette of blue, purple and mauve. The yarn ends are knotted into a fringe.

Shawls, ponchos and wraps

Highly fashionable and popular, crochet shawls, ponchos and wraps can take many forms. From a lacy evening accessory to a snug winter warmer. Explore the many possible methods of construction from using freeform crochet pieces to working a lacy stitch all over, and to adding fringes and textures.

▶ **TEXTURED PONCHO**
Margaret Hubert

Crocheted in a multicoloured novelty yarn, this fun poncho is decorated with crochet flowers and fringed with lengths of yarn mixed with strips of chiffon fabric

◀ **LACY SHAWL**
Jennifer Hansen

Worked from the point upwards, this versatile shawl is cleverly shaped so that it sits neatly on the shoulders. Great as casual wear with blue jeans and a T-shirt during the day, it looks dressy for the evening draped over a strapless top and matching tailored trousers.

▲ LACY SHAWL

This delightful lacy shawl is made of flower motifs joined together, and shows how light and delicate a piece of crochet can be. The shawl is trimmed with a generously deep knotted fringe.

▶ FREEFORM PONCHO
Margaret Hubert

Worked by joining pieces of crochet while changing yarns, stitches and colours, this freeform poncho combines a huge range of textures and stitch patterns.

Crochet in the home

Crochet is a very versatile technique for making home accessories, particularly those on a large scale such as afghans, blankets and throws which can easily be made in one piece. Square, round and hexagonal motifs combine well to make cushion covers and throws which will add interest to any home decor.

▲ SPIRAL EXPLORATION
Jennifer Hansen

This cushion cover was originally designed as a freeform exercise in exploring, constructing and combining spiral shapes. The choice of colours is interesting; careful use of cool and hot colours accentuate the spiral effect.

◀ SOFTLY TEXTURED THROW
Carol Meldrum

Worked throughout in treble crochet, this rectangular lambswool and mohair throw is bordered with a chunky fringe made from thick merino wool in a contrasting colour.

◀ LACY CUSHIONS

Crochet cushion covers worked in cream or white cotton yarn can look very effective grouped together on a sofa or daybed, especially in a room with country cottage-style decor.

▼ FUNKY FLOOR CUSHION
Carol Meldrum

Constructed from four panels using a controlled sequence of rotating coloured stripes, the front of this floor cushion worked in treble crochet shows how effective good colour choices can look.

Jewellery

Crocheted jewellery has emerged in recent years as a versatile and distinctive fashion statement. Currently seen in accessory shops and on the catwalk, jewellery can be crocheted from either conventional yarns or from sterling silver and pliable craft wire. It can be as simple as a pretty flower pin or as elaborate as a multi-stranded necklace decorated with beads.

▸ **CASCADE**
Jenny Dowde

Crocheted in 28-tension craft wire threaded with a variety of beads in pastel shades of purple and turquoise, this delicate necklace was created with just two crochet stitches, double and treble crochet.

◀ **CIRCULAR DISC NECKLACE**
Carol Meldrum

Created from a series of circular motifs suspended from a metallic chain, this eye-catching necklace is the perfect fashion accessory to wear with a light summer dress.

◀ ▾ **FLORAL MOTIFS**
Jennifer Hansen

Flower motifs can be used as pins and corsages, or attached to bracelets and necklaces. Spider bud (left) features popcorn stitches; Marguerite (below centre) uses progressively taller stitches to make a star shape and Lupi-flora (bottom right) combines loop stitches with double crochet.

▲ DELICATE BEADED BRACELET
Carol Meldrum

Crocheted in a fine but durable gold jewellery wire with the addition of varying sizes of beads in shades of green and grey, this delightful bracelet is worked in double crochet.

◀ BOBBLE NECKLACES
A Colecionadora

This fantastic neck decoration is made from lengths of crochet studded with textured bobbles. The colours are delightful; they range from cranberry to hot scarlet and fuchsia, right through to palest shell pink.

Bags

Crochet is the perfect technique for making purses, bags and totes as it makes a strong, substantial fabric which will keep its shape well in wear. Worked in the round or in separate pieces, a crochet bag provides the perfect opportunity for making small-scale experiments with colour, different types of yarns and textures.

▲ FANTASY GARDEN
Jenny Dowde

This bag was made by crocheting hand-sized pieces in a variety of basic stitches such as double, treble, and double treble crochet interspersed with textural stitches, including bobbles. The pieces were then assembled and hand-stitched together.

▲ CAT BAG
Carol Ventura

Worked in the round using double crochet, this bag is worked in a multicoloured crochet technique known as tapestry crochet which originated in Guatemala and areas of South America.

◄ ZIGZAG BAG
Carol Meldrum

Bright, funky colours accentuate the zigzag pattern on the front of this crochet bag with bamboo handles. The pattern is created by working rows of spike stitches on a double crochet background.

Dolls and toys

Soft woolly toys and dressed dolls have always been favourite playthings for young children. Worked in fine yarns, crochet can make wonderful outfits to dress new and vintage dolls, and is good for making stuffed toys such as teddy bears and other animals in a wide range of styles.

◀ FUZZBUTT RABBIT
Dennis Hansbury and Denika Robbins

Japanese "Amigurumi" style soft toys are crocheted in the round using double crochet and stuffed firmly so they hold their shape. Fuzzbutt rabbit has glass doll eyes and a simple embroidered mouth.

▲ DRESSED DOLL
Drew Emborsky

The designer has dressed a vintage doll from 1949 in a ruffled crochet dress complete with lacy petticoats and matching picture hat. Worked in sport weight baby yarn, the garment used double, half treble and treble crochet stitches.

◀ BINKY RABBIT
Dennis Hansbury and Denika Robbins

Another stuffed toy in the popular Japanese "Amigurumi" style, Binky rabbit features the non-matching eyes and characteristically deadpan expression common to this style.

CARE OF CROCHET

Following a few simple guidelines while you are working will keep your pieces of crochet looking fresh and clean during the making process. Once a project is completed, it's important always to follow the yarn manufacturer's laundering instructions and to store crocheted pieces carefully and appropriately.

WORKING GUIDELINES

Always wash your hands thoroughly before starting to crochet and avoid using hand cream as the oils in the cream may transfer to the yarn. When crocheting with light-coloured yarns, try to avoid wearing dark-coloured garments that shed "bits" while you are working – angora or mohair jumpers are the worst as they shed tiny hairs which get trapped in your work. Getting cat and dog hairs on your crochet is also best avoided as they are difficult to remove.

When you've finished making a crochet project, store a small amount of left-over yarn from each project carefully, just in case you need to make repairs in the future. You can wind a length of yarn round a piece of card, making a note of the yarn type and colour as well as details of the project. It's also a good idea to attach one of the ball bands from the yarn as this will remind you of the yarn composition and any special pressing and laundering instructions. File the cards neatly away in a dust-proof box, and store in a cool, dry place.

LOOKING AFTER CROCHET

Follow the laundering and pressing instructions on the ball band for the particular yarn you have used. More information on ball bands is given on page 20. If the yarn you have used is machine-washable, put the item into a zip-up mesh laundry bag to prevent stretching and snagging during the wash cycle. If you don't have a mesh bag, you can use an old, clean white pillowcase instead; simply secure the open end with an elastic hair band or work a row of running stitches across the opening to close the pillowcase. If you have household items such as tablecloths or tray cloths trimmed with crochet, treat spills and stains as soon as they occur and repair any damage to the crochet fabric before laundering the item.

For crochet pieces made from yarns which are not machine-washable, wash carefully by hand in hand-hot water with a mild, detergent-free cleaning agent. Most specialist wool or fabric shampoos are ideal, but check that the one you choose does not contain optical brighteners which will cause yarn colours to fade. Rinse the piece thoroughly in several changes of water the same temperature as the washing water to avoid felting. Carefully squeeze as much surplus water out as you can, without wringing, then roll the damp item in a towel and press to remove more moisture. Gently ease the item into shape and dry flat out of direct sunlight. Follow the instructions on the ball band for pressing once the item is dry.

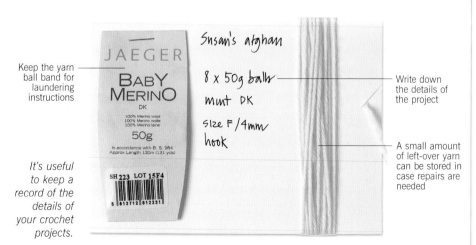

Keep the yarn ball band for laundering instructions

It's useful to keep a record of the details of your crochet projects.

Susan's afghan

8 x 50g balls

mint DK

size F/4mm hook

Write down the details of the project

A small amount of left-over yarn can be stored in case repairs are needed

HAND WASHING	MACHINE WASHING	BLEACHING	PRESSING	DRY CLEANING
Do not wash by hand or machine	Machine washable in warm water at stated temperature	Bleaching not permitted	Do not press	Do not dry clean
Hand washable in warm water at stated temperature	Machine washable in warm water at stated temperature, cool rinse and short spin	Bleaching permitted (with chlorine)	Press with a cool iron	May be dry cleaned with all solutions
	Machine washable in warm water at stated temperature, short spin		Press with a warm iron	May be dry cleaned with perchlorethylene or fluorocarbon or petroleum-based solvents
			Press with a hot iron	May be dry cleaned with fluorocarbon or petroleum-based solvents only

Always check the yarn ball band for washing and pressing instructions. Standard laundering symbols as used on ball bands can be seen left.

STORING CROCHET

The main enemies of crochet fabrics –apart from dust and dirt – are direct sunlight, which can cause yarn colours to fade and fibres to weaken; excess heat which makes yarn dry and brittle; damp, which rots fibres, and moths which can seriously damage woollen yarns. Avoid storing yarns or finished crochet items for any length of time in polythene bags as the polythene attracts dirt and dust, which will transfer readily to your work. Polythene also prevents yarns containing natural fibres such as cotton and linen from breathing which can result in mildew attacks and eventually weaken or rot the fibres. Instead, store small items wrapped in white, acid-free tissue paper or an old cotton pillowcase. For large, heavy items such as winter-weight jackets and sweaters, which might drop and stretch out of shape if stored on coat hangers, fold them loosely between layers of white tissue paper, making sure that each fold is padded with tissue. Store all the items in a drawer, cupboard or other dark, dry and moth-free place and check them regularly, refolding larger items. It's also a good idea to make small fabric bags filled with dried lavender flowers and tuck them into the drawer or cupboard with your crochet as the smell deters moths.

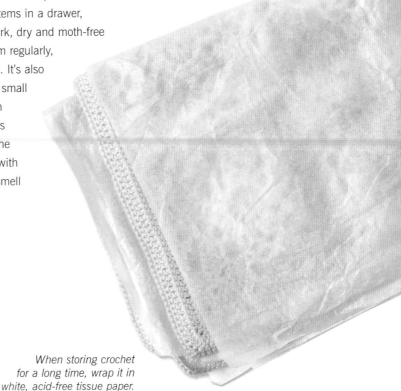

When storing crochet for a long time, wrap it in white, acid-free tissue paper.

ABBREVIATIONS AND SYMBOLS

These are the abbreviations and symbols used in this book. There is no worldwide standard, so in other publications you may find different abbreviations and symbols.

STANDARD CROCHET ABBREVIATIONS

alt	alternate
beg	beginning
ch(s)	chain(s)
cont	continue
dc	double crochet
foll	following
htr	half treble crochet
lp(s)	loop(s)
patt	pattern
RS	right side
rem	remaining
rep	repeat
sk	skip
sl st	slip stitch
sp(s)	space(s)
st(s)	stitch(es)
tr	treble or triple crochet
WS	wrong side
yo	wrap yarn over hook

STITCH SYMBOLS

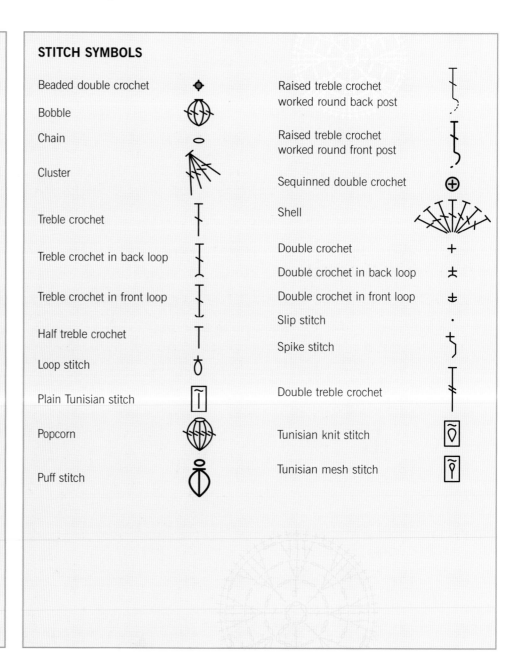

Beaded double crochet	
Bobble	
Chain	
Cluster	
Treble crochet	
Treble crochet in back loop	
Treble crochet in front loop	
Half treble crochet	
Loop stitch	
Plain Tunisian stitch	
Popcorn	
Puff stitch	

Raised treble crochet worked round back post	
Raised treble crochet worked round front post	
Sequinned double crochet	
Shell	
Double crochet	
Double crochet in back loop	
Double crochet in front loop	
Slip stitch	
Spike stitch	
Double treble crochet	
Tunisian knit stitch	
Tunisian mesh stitch	

ADDITIONAL SYMBOLS

Change colour

Direction of working →

Do not turn

Fasten off ◀

Foundation row F R

Join in new colour ◁

ENGLISH/AMERICAN TERMINOLOGY

The patterns in this book use English terminology. Patterns published using American terminology can be very confusing because some American terms differ from the English system, as shown below:

English	American
double crochet (dc)	single crochet (sc)
extended double (exdc)	extended single crochet (exsc)
half treble crochet (htr)	half double crochet (hdc)
treble crochet (tr)	double crochet (dc)
double treble crochet (dtr)	treble crochet (tr)
triple treble crochet (trtr or ttr)	double treble crochet (dtr)

ARRANGEMENTS OF SYMBOLS

Description	Symbol	Explanation
symbols joined at top	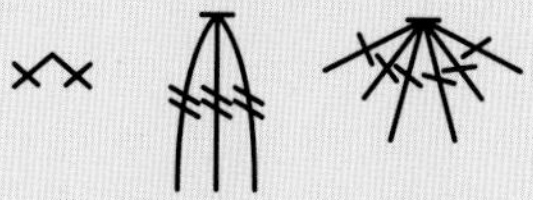	A group of symbols may be joined at the top, indicating that these stitches should be worked together as a cluster
symbols joined at base		Symbols joined at the base should all be worked into the same stitch below
symbols joined at top and bottom		Sometimes a group of stitches is joined at both top and bottom, making a puff, bobble or popcorn
symbols on a curve		Sometimes symbols are drawn along a curve, depending on the construction of the stitch pattern
distorted symbols		Some symbols may be lengthened, curved or spiked to indicate where the hook is inserted below, as for spike stitches

CATEGORIES OF YARN, TENSION RANGES AND RECOMMENDED HOOK SIZES

Yarn weight category	Super fine	Fine	Light	Medium	Bulky	Super bulky
Type of yarns in category	Sock, fingering, baby	Sport, baby	DK, light worsted	Worsted, afghan, aran	Chunky, craft, rug	Bulky, roving
Crochet tension ranges in double crochet to 10 cm (4 in)	23–32 sts	16–20 sts	12–17 sts	11–14 sts	8–11 sts	5–9 sts
Recommended hook in metric size range	2.25–3.5 mm	3.5–4.5 mm	4.5–5.5 mm	5.5–6.5 mm	6.5–9 mm	9 mm and larger
Recommended hook US size range	B–1 to E–4	E–4 to 7	7 to I–9	I–9 to K–10 ½	K–10 ½ to M–13	M–13 and larger

The above reflect the most commonly used tensions and needle or hook sizes for specific yarn categories.

Super fine

Medium

Bulky

Fine

Light

Super bulky

Crochet hooks are available in a wide range of sizes, shapes and materials.

GLOSSARY

Ball band
The paper strip or paper tag on a ball or skein of yarn. A ball band gives information about weight, shade number, dye lot number and fibre content of the yarn. It may also show care instructions and other details, including yardage and suggested tension and hook size.

Blocking
Setting a piece of crochet by stretching and pinning it out on a flat surface before steaming or treating with cold water.

Bobble
Several stitches worked in the same place and joined together at the top to make a decorative raised bump. Bobbles are often worked on a background of shorter stitches.

Border
A deep, decorative strip of crochet, usually worked with one straight and one shaped edge that is used for trimming pieces of crochet or fabric.

Braid
A narrow, decorative strip of crochet similar in appearance to a purchased furnishing braid.

Broomstick crochet
A particular type of crochet, worked with both a crochet hook and a "broomstick" such as a large knitting needle.

Chain space
Space formed by working lengths of chain stitches between other stitches. Also known as chain loops or chain arches.

Cluster
Several incomplete stitches worked together so they join at the top.

Decrease
Removing one or more stitches to reduce the number of working stitches.

Dye lot
The batch of dye used for a specific ball of yarn. Shades can vary between batches, so always use yarn from the same dye lot to make an item.

Edge finish
A decorative crochet edging worked directly into the edge of a piece of crochet.

Edging
A narrow strip of crochet, usually with one straight and one shaped edge, used for trimming pieces of crochet or fabric.

Fan
Several stitches worked into the same chain or stitch which make a fan, or shell, shape.

Fibre
Natural or manmade substances spun together to make yarn.

Filet crochet
Filet crochet patterns are worked solidly and set against a regularly worked mesh background. Filet crochet is usually worked from a graphic chart rather than written instructions.

Foundation chain
A length of chain stitches that forms the base for a piece of crochet.

Foundation row
In a stitch pattern, the first row worked into the foundation chain. The foundation row is not repeated as part of the pattern.

Heading
Extra rows of plain crochet worked on the long straight edge of an edging or border to add strength and durability.

Increase
Adding one or more stitches to increase the number of working stitches.

Intarsia
Intarsia produces a design featuring areas of different colours which are each worked with a separate small ball of yarn. Intarsia patterns are worked in two or more colours from a coloured chart on a grid. Each coloured square on the chart represents one stitch.

Jacquard
Jacquard patterns are similar to intarsia, but the yarns are continued along the row rather than being used separately. A Jacquard pattern is shown as a coloured chart on a grid. Each coloured square on the chart represents one stitch.

Lace
A stitch pattern forming an openwork design similar in appearance to lace fabric.

Mesh
A stitch pattern forming a regular geometric grid.

Motif
A shaped piece of crochet, often worked in rounds. Several motifs can be joined together rather like fabric patchwork to make a larger piece. Also known as a medallion or block.

Pattern
A set of instructions showing exactly how to make a garment or other crochet item.

Pattern repeat
The specific number of rows or rounds that are needed to complete one stitch pattern.

Picot
A decorative chain space often closed into a ring with a slip stitch. The number of chains in a picot can vary.

Ply
A single strand of yarn made by twisting fibres together. Most yarn is made from two or more plies twisted together to make different yarn weights, although some woollen yarns are made from a single thick ply.

Puff
Several half treble crochet stitches worked in the same place, and joined together at the top to make a raised stitch.

Right side
The front of crochet fabric. This side is usually visible on a finished item, although some stitch patterns may be reversible.

Round
A row of crochet worked in the round; the end of one round is joined to the beginning of the same round. Rounds of crochet can form flat motifs or tubular shapes.

Row
A line of stitches worked from side to side to make a flat piece of crochet.

Seam
The join made where two pieces of crochet are stitched or crocheted together.

Sewing needle
A needle with a sharp point used for applying a crochet braid, edging or border to a piece of fabric.

Spike
A decorative stitch worked by inserting the hook from front to back of the work, one or more rows below the normal position, and/or to the right or left of the working stitch.

Starting chain
A specific number of chain stitches worked at the beginning of a round to bring the hook up to the correct height for the next stitch that is being worked.

Stitch pattern
A sequence or combination of crochet stitches that is repeated over and over again to create a piece of crochet fabric.

Surface crochet
Rows of decorative crochet worked on top of a crochet background.

Symbol chart
Charts that describe a crochet pattern visually, by using symbols to indicate the different stitches and exactly where and how they should be placed in relation to one another.

Tapestry needle
A large, blunt-ended embroidery needle used for sewing pieces of crochet together.

Tension
The looseness or tightness of a crochet fabric expressed as a specific number of rows and stitches in a given area, usually 10 cm (4 in) square.

Trim
A length of crochet worked separately and sewn to a main piece, or onto plain fabric, as a decoration.

Tunisian crochet
A particular type of crochet worked with a special long hook. Tunisian crochet is worked back and forth in rows without turning the work.

Turning chain
A specific number of chain stitches worked at the beginning of a row to bring the hook up to the correct height for the next stitch that is being worked.

Wrong side
The reverse side of crochet fabric; this side is not usually visible on a finished item.

Yarn needle
A very large blunt-pointed needle used for sewing pieces of crochet together.

SUPPLIERS

ENGLAND

NORTH EAST

Burn & Walton
Parkside Place
Bellingham
Hexham NE48 2AY
01434 220 395
burnwalton@aol.com

Ring a Rosie
69 Front Street
Monkseaton
Whitley Bay
Tyne and Wear NE25 8AA
0191 252 8874

The Wool Shop
13 Castlegate
Berwick upon Tweed
TD15 1JS
01289 306 104

NORTH WEST

And Sew What
247 Eaves Lane
Chorley
Lancashire PR6 0AG
01257 267 438
www.sewwhat.gb.com

Marchmoon Limited
73 Avondale Road
Liverpool L15 3HF
01704 577 415

Spinning a Yarn
46 Market Street
Ulverston
Cumbria LA12 7LS
01229 581 020
www.spinningayarn.com

Stash
4 Godstall Lane
Chester
Cheshire CH1 1LN
01244 311 136
www.celticove.com

Victoria Grant
Waterways
High Street
Uppermill
Oldham
Lancashire OL3 6HT
01457 870 756

YORKSHIRE

Attica 2
Commercial Street
Hebden Bridge
West Yorkshire HX7 8AJ

Bobbins
Wesley Hall
Church Street
Whitby
North Yorkshire YO22 4DE
01947 600 585

Busy Hands
Unit 16 Ashbrook Park
Parkside Lane
Leeds LS11 5SF
0113 272 0851

Jenny Scott's Creative Embroidery
The Old Post Office
39 Duke Street
Settle
North Yorkshire BD24 9DJ
01729 824 298

WEST MIDLANDS

Cucumberpatch Limited
13 March Avenue
Wolstanton
Newcastle under Lyme
Staffordshire ST5 8BB
01782 878 234
www.cucumberpatch.co.uk

K2Tog
97 High Street
Wolstanton
Newcastle under Lyme
Staffordshire ST5 0EP
01782 862 332

Web of Wool
53 Regent Grove
Holly Walk
Leamington Spa
Warwick CV32 4PA
01926 311 614

EAST MIDLANDS

Bee Inspired Limited
The Old Post Office
236 Windmill Avenue
Kettering
Northamptonshire
NN1 7DQ
01536 514 646

Heirs and Graces
The Square
Bakewell
Derbyshire DE45 1DA
01629 815 873

The Knitting Workshop
23 Trowell Grove
Long Eaton
Nottingham NG10 4A
0115 946 8370

Quorn Country Crafts
18 Churchgate
Loughborough
Leicestershire LE11 1UD
01509 211 604

Taylor's Teddies
4a Graham Road
Great Malvern
Worcestershire WR14 2HN
01684 572 760

EAST ANGLIA

Arts & Crafts
Tunstead Road
Hoveton
Wroxham
Norfolk NR12 8QG
01603 783 505

D & P Colchester
The Barn
South Lodge Farm
Low Road
Great Plumstead
Norwich
Norfolk NR13 5ED
01603 721 466

Sew Creative
97 King Street
Cambridge CB1 1LD
01223 350 691

SOUTH EAST

Battle Wool Shop
2 Mount Street
Battle
East Sussex TN33 0EG
01424 775 073

Gades
Victoria Plaza
242 Churchill South
Southend on Sea
Essex SS2 5SD
01702 613 789

The Knit Tin
2 Fountain Court
Olney
Buckinghamshire
MK46 4BB
01234 714 300

Loop
41 Cross Street
Islington
London N1 2BB
020 7288 1160
www.loop.gb.com

Myfanwy Hart
Winifred Cottage
17 Elms Road
Fleet
Hampshire GU15 3EG
01252 617 667

Pandora
196 High Street
Guildford
Surrey GU1 3HZ
01483 572 558
www.stitch1knit1.com

Portmeadow Designs
104 Walton Street
Oxford
Oxfordshire OX2 6EB
01865 311 008

Shoreham Knitting & Needlecraft
19 East Street
Shoreham-by-Sea
West Sussex BN43 5ZE
01273 461 029
www.englishyarns.co.uk

Taj Yarn & Crafts
2 Wellesey Avenue
Richings Park
Iver
Buckinghamshire S10 9AY
01753 653 900

Yummies
91 Queens Park Road
Brighton
East Sussex BN2 0GJ
01273 672 632

SOUTH WEST
Divine Design
Libra Court
Fore Street
Sidmouth
Devon EX10 8AJ
07967 127 273

Knitting Corner
9 Pepper Street
149–150 East Reach
Taunton
Somerset TA1 3HT
01823 284 768

Sally Carr Designs
The Yarn Shop
31 High Street
Totnes
Devon TQ9 5NP
01803 863 060

WALES

B's Hive
20–22 Church Street
Monmouth
Gwent NP25 3BU
01600 713 548

Clare's
13 Great Darkgate Street
Aberystwyth SY23 1DE
01970 617 786

Copperfield
Four Mile Bridge Road
Valley
Anglesey LL65 3HV
01407 740 982

Mrs Mac's
2 Woodville Road
Mumbles
Swansea SA3 4AD
01792 369 820

SCOTLAND

CE Cross Stitch
Narvik
Weyland Terrace
Kirkwall
Orkney KW15 1LS
01856 879 049

Cormack's and Crawford's
56–57 High Street
Dingwall
Ross-shire IV15 9HL
01349 562 234

Di Gilpin
Hansa Close
Burghers Close
141 South Street
St Andrews
Fife KY16 9UN
01334 476 193
www.handknitwear.com

Elizabeth Lovick
Harbour View
Front Road
Orkney KW17 2SL
01603 783 505

Galloway Knitwear
6 Manx View
Port William
Dumfries & Galloway
DG8 9SA
01988 700 789

HK Handknit
83 Bruntsfield Place
Edinburgh EH10 4HG
0131 228 1551
www.handknit.co.uk

Hume Sweet Hume
Pierowall Village
Westray
Orkney KW17 2DH
01857 677 259

The Knitting Parlour
The Park
Findliorn Bay
Forres
Moray IV36 0TZ
01684 527 760

Patterns of Light
Kishorn
Strathcarron
Wester-ross IV54 8XB
01520 733 363

Pie in the Skye
Ferry View, Armadale Bay
Sleat
Isle of Skye IV45 8RS
01471 844 370

Ragamuffin
278 Canon Gate
The Royal Mile
Edinburgh EH8 8AA
0131 557 6007

Twist Fibre Craft Studio
88 High Street
Newburgh
Cupar
Fife KY14 6AQ
01337 842 843
www.twistfibrecraft.co.uk

Victoria Gibson
The Esplanade
Lerwick
Shetland ZE1 0LL
01595 692 816

The Wool Shed
Alford Heritage Centre
Mart Road
Alford
Aberdeenshire AB33 8BZ
01975 562 906

Wooly Ewe
7 Abbey Court
Kelso
Berwickshire TD5 7JA
01573 225 889

NORTHERN IRELAND

Coolwoolz
46 Mill Hill
Warringstown
County Down BT66 7QP
02838 820 202

AUSTRALIA

Calico & Ivy
1 Glyde Street
Mosman Park, WA 6012
08 9383 3794
www.calicohouse.com.au
calicohs@ozemail.com.au

Cleckheaton
Australian Country Spinners
314 Albert Street
Brunswick, VIC 3056
03 9380 3888
www.cleckheaton.biz

The Knitting Loft
PO Box 266
Tunstall Square
East Doncaster, VIC 3109
03 9841 4818
www.knittingloft.com
sales@knittingloft.com

The Shearing Shed
Shop 7B
Manuka Court
Bougainville Street
Manuka
Canberra, ACT 2603
02 6295 0061
www.theshearingshed.com.au

Sunspin
185 Canterbury Road
Canterbury
Melbourne, VIC 3126
03 9830 1609
www.sunspun.com.au
shop@sunspun.com.au

Tapestry Craft
50 York Street
Sydney, NSW 2000
02 9299 8588
www.tapestrycraft.com.au

Threads and More
141 Boundary Road
Bardon, QLD 4065
07 3367 0864
www.threadsandmore.
com.au
shop@threadsandmore.
com.au

Wool Baa
124 Bridport Street
Albert Park, VIC 3207
03 9690 6633
www.woolbaa.com.au
sales@woolbaa.com.au

The Wool Shack
PO Box 228
Innaloo City
Perth, WA 6918
08 9446 6344
www.thewoolshack.com
info@thewoolshack.com

Xotix Yarns
PO Box 1636
Kingscliff, NSW 2487
02 6677 7241
www.xotixyarns.com.au

Yarns Galore
5/25 Queens Road
Mount Pleasant, WA 6153
08 9315 3070
http://yarnsgalore.com.au

NEW ZEALAND

Accessories Stories Ltd
407 Cuba Street
Lower Hutt
Wellington
04 587 0004
www.woolworks.org

Alterknitives
PO Box 47961
Auckland
09 376 0337

Anny Blatt Handknitting Yarns
PO Box 65364
Mairangi Bay
Auckland
09 479 2043

Busy Needles
73B Victoria Street
Cambridge

Dyepot
Accent Fibres
1084 Maraekakaho Road
R.D.5
Hastings
Hawkes Bay
06 876 4233
www.dyepot.co.nz
Sheryl@dyepot.co.nz

John Q Goldingham
PO Box 45083
Epuni
Lower Hutt
04 567 4085

Knit World
189 Peterborough Street
Christchurch
03 379 2300
knitting@xtra.co.nz

Knit World
26 The Octagon
Dunedin 9001
03 477 0400

Knit World
Shop 210b
Left Bank
Cuba Mall
Wellington
04 385 1918

The Stitchery
Suncourt Shopping Centre
Tamamuta Street
Taupo
07 378 9195
stitchery@xtra.co.nz

Treliske Organic Wools
2RD Roxburgh
Central Otago
03 446 6828
info@treliskeorganic.com

Wool 'n' Things
109 New Brighton Mall
New Brighton
Christchurch
03 388 3391

Wool World
26 Kelvin Street
Invercargill
03 218 8217

Yarn Barn
179 Burnett Street
Ashburton
03 308 6243

WEB RESOURCES

The Craft Yarn Council: www.craftyarncouncil.com
The Crochet Guild of America: www.crochet.org
Craft Australia: www.craftaus.com.au

SELECTED SUPPLIERS

www.buy-mail.co.uk
www.coatscrafts.co.uk
www.colourway.co.uk
www.coolwoolz.co.uk
www.designeryarns.uk.com
www.diamondyarns.com
www.ethknits.co.uk
www.e-yarn.com
www.handworksgallery.com
www.hantex.co.uk
www.hook-n-needle.com
www.kangaroo.uk.com
www.karpstyles.ca
www.kgctrading.com
www.knitrowan.com
www.knittersdream.com/yarn
www.knittingfever.com
www.knitwellwools.co.uk
www.lacis.com
www.maggiescrochet.com
www.mcadirect.com
www.patternworks.com
www.patonsyarns.com
www.personalthreads.com
www.sakonnetpurls.com
www.shetland-wool-brokers-zetnet.co.uk
www.sirdar.co.uk
www.spiningayarn.com
www.theknittinggarden.com
www.upcountry.co.uk
www.yarncompany.com
www.yarnexpressions.com
www.yarnmarket.com

INDEX

CREDITS

Quarto would like to thank the contributing artists for kindly supplying images reproduced in this book. Artists are acknowledged beside their work.

ARTIST'S WEBSITES

Dennis Hansbury and Denika Robbins
www.vagrantaesthetic.com

Jenny Dowde
www.jennydowde.com

Drew Emborsky
www.thecrochetdude.biz

Yoko Hatta
www.kazekobo.net

Jennifer Hansen
www.stitchdiva.com

Margaret Hubert
www.margarethubertoriginals.com

Carol Meldrum
www.beatknit.co.uk

Lajla Nuhic
www.lajla.ca

Kristin Omdahl
www.styledbykristin.com

Carol Ventura
www.tapestrycrochet.com

Quarto would also like to acknowledge the following:

Key: l = left, r = right

143l © GETTY IMAGES
141l © MICHAEL BOYS / CORBIS
139l © DEBORAH JAFFE / STONE+ / GETTY IMAGES
135l, 135r © NICHON VOGUE CO., LTD

Thanks also to the models – Isabelle Crawford and Kryssy Moss.

All other photographs and illustrations are the copyright of Quarto Publishing plc. While every effort has been made to credit contributors, Quarto would like to apologize should there have been any omissions or errors – and would be pleased to make the appropriate correction for future editions of the book.